e-shock 2020

e-shock 2020

How the Digital Technology Revolution Is Changing Business and All Our Lives

Michael de Kare-Silver

Best-selling author, digital technology/e-commerce advisor and team-builder

palgrave
macmillan

First published 2011 by
PALGRAVE MACMILLAN

Palgrave Macmillan in the UK is an imprint of Macmillan Publishers Limited, registered in England, company number 785998, of Houndmills, Basingstoke, Hampshire RG21 6XS.

Palgrave Macmillan in the US is a division of St Martin's Press LLC, 175 Fifth Avenue, New York, NY 10010.

Palgrave Macmillan is the global academic imprint of the above companies and has companies and representatives throughout the world.

Palgrave® and Macmillan® are registered trademarks in the United States, the United Kingdom, Europe and other countries

ISBN-13: 978-0-230-30130-6

This book is printed on paper suitable for recycling and made from fully managed and sustained forest sources. Logging, pulping and manufacturing processes are expected to conform to the environmental regulations of the country of origin.

A catalogue record for this book is available from the British Library.

A catalog record for this book is available from the Library of Congress.

10 9 8 7 6 5 4 3 2 1
20 19 18 17 16 15 14 13 12 11

Printed and bound in Great Britain by
CPI Antony Rowe, Chippenham and Eastbourne

To Deborah and Alexander, my inspirations!

Contents

1 The Technology Revolution

There is a truly disruptive but exhilarating revolution taking place. Technology has moved into a new era. Digital is changing the way we communicate, the way we buy things, the way businesses interact, the way we talk. Our expectations of what we can do and how we can do it have been transformed. The "I-want-it-now", time-poor, technically-literate developed world now demands the convenience of being able to do things "my way". I want the anytime, anyhow, anywhere world. I rely on it. It governs my life

There's a complete transformation taking place. Technically we've moved at an incredibly rapid pace in the past 30 years. We could say we're now in the sixth stage of recent evolution:

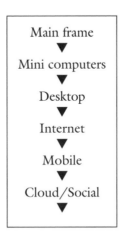

Main frame
▼
Mini computers
▼
Desktop
▼
Internet
▼
Mobile
▼
Cloud/Social
▼

The pace of these developments, as observed in a Morgan Stanley report, has accelerated. If mainframes took some 20 years to reach mass commercialization, mobile has taken about 7 and social has taken about 3. Whether you talk Moore's Law or more simply the billions of dollars of private equity investment, there is a huge amount of continuing R&D and an absolute wealth of ideas in the pipeline of new products that are all queuing and lining-up to find their own commercial, life-changing, business breakthrough applications.

Where is all this heading? What are we likely to see as this decade unfolds? Can we even begin to imagine our world in 2020? Who could have predicted the current scene? Who would have imagined that traditional business models would be so much under threat? Who could have predicted Facebook or the dominance of Apple and Google? Who could have foreseen that online commerce would have destroyed bricks 'n mortar book shops, record shops, video hire, changed forever the way we buy travel and insurance, the way we bank, buy clothes and electricals, expanded our ability to search the world for bargains, the ease with which a business in London can find customers in China (and more typically the other way around!). The beginning of the 20th century saw the demise of old cotton mills and the collapse of manufacturing in the West as we gained access to lower wage costs and lower prices in Asia. We look back at some of these historic changes and ask: Why didn't the big companies of the day move with the times? Why did great businesses become dinosaurs? And we wonder which great corporations of now will become the dinosaurs of tomorrow. Will companies like Microsoft for example continue to have such a vice-like grip on computer operating systems? If the trend to mobile internet access and mobile computing continues, then might the leading OS from Blackberry, Apple and Google Android supplant that Seattle monolith?

Just twenty years ago mostly the only computers that were in use were in corporations and even then most people did not have one on their desktop. Now they are everywhere and the way we interact with them has fundamentally changed. Human beings think they are in control. But are we? We have become completely dependent on digital machines and equipment. We rely on them completely. Without them we are lost. If we lose our mobile we are distraught. In one recent survey, the one thing people said that they would be most upset about losing was their mobile. It ranked higher than the credit card, jewelry, the car and even the pet dog or cat! – "it is my most treasured possession."

And we are all expecting computing use, access and application to continue to develop and improve. We can now access them 24/7 from most anywhere. It used to be a world of point and click, now we touch and it's like simply pressing a button. Already many people talk to their computer, and voice command and voice recognition software is improving all the time. How much longer before the computer talks to us? Such technology already exists. The computer (can be programmed) to switch itself on at say 6.30am, give us our wake-up call and offer a cheery Good Morning in whatever tone of voice we have selected. As we're getting showered and dressed it can be telling us about our schedule for the day. We can say "book taxi" and (through a simple pre-program and computer Q&A) confirm location and time. We can voice emails and text messages. We can even send through a repeat shopping order. We can tell our computer to schedule a delivery next time we're home, book a restaurant, arrange our travel – do anything which can be reduced down to automated digital communications. How soon before this sort of interaction and expectation becomes the norm? In fact have computers already taken control? Here are a few recent headlines:

> "Algorithms take control of Wall Street" (Wired.com)
>
> "Computer program allows car to stay in its lane without human control" (*Science Daily*)
>
> "Computers 'to replace teachers'" (*Daily Telegraph*)
>
> "Will techology take over the world?" (Helium.com)
>
> "When will computer hardware match the human brain … in the 2020s" (*Journal of Evolution and Technology*)

In the novel *Nine Tomorrows* Isaac Asimov portrays a futuristic world where computers do control humans. Asimov describes how humans become dependent. No need to read books or study. Why bother when the computer already has that knowledge and you can access it when you want? Just rely on computers! Computers start to select from their vast store of knowledge what to teach humans. They make their own priorities and start shaping what humans know. They start to keep some knowledge away from humans and just for their own data banks, for themselves. Computers start to control humans' lives.

Far-fetched? While Asimov is critical of this future dependency, we are already close to it. Google's algorithms decide what we see and in what order we see it. Medical diagnostic software tells physicians what the problem is and what treatment is required. Traffic control systems automatically regulate air traffic and auto routes. Our old-fashioned "Point and Click" world, where we controlled what we would look at, is quickly morphing into a two-way "Touch and Talk". It won't be long before we expect the computer to start learning about us: recognize our voice, anticipate our regular commands. As we stop needing to stare at a screen then our desire for continued "screenless", interactive, intelligent communication can take us into a Stephen Spielberg/Tom Cruise "Minority Report"-type world where what 10 years ago was pure science fiction becomes a reality.

Who will be the companies that are the providers of these applications and solutions? Who are the new kids on the block? What seems to be happening is that, in our new world, smaller more agile companies have the best chance to succeed. They can access the funds (at least if they're on the US West Coast they can … try getting true venture capital in Europe!), they can leverage remote but global partnerships, they can interact and share work-in-progress easily and cost-effectively. Tech start-ups will be all the rage. Here are a few examples of top 100 tech companies from Innovation.com.

▷ **Anboto** provides technological solutions to enable an easy and smart interaction in natural language between customers and computers.

▷ **Natural User Interface Technologies (NUITEQ)** is a Swedish multi-touch software technology company, which enables people to engage with touch screens using multiple fingers simultaneously.

▷ **Canatu Oy**'s business is the production of a new class of versatile components based on carbon nanotubes. These components improve the performance and reduce the cost of optical energy generation and storage and electrical devices while, simultaneously, reducing their environmental footprint.

▷ Semaphore from **Smart Logic** is an innovative tool in taxonomy management and automatic knowledge classification. It builds the connections between topics, entities and resources. This semantic intelligence enables users to quickly manage, find, explore and use content.

▷ **ID-U** offers a new concept in biometric identification. It is the first stimuli-driven biometric system. The technology is based on the uniqueness of a person's eye-movement patterns. Utilization of a user's kinetic response to construct his identification signature is called 4D-Biometrics.

Others, like Groupon, Foursquare, Layar, Tumblr, Zynga and Spotify which have a strong B2C orientation, have quickly gained traction and are also discussed later.

Alongside the on-going march of technology innovation, there are a number of big transformation themes that are going to shape this decade.

(i)   The rise of the MCE, the Multi-Channel Enterprise.

(ii)   The demise of the traditional bricks 'n mortar retailer model.

(iii) The development of major new online distributors and intermediaries for products and services, replacing the Tescos and Wal-Marts of the old world.

(iv)   Human computer interaction will change from "point and click" to a world of "think talk move".

(v)   The shift from "push" advertising and marketing to "pull" user-generated buzz.

(vi)   The need for major "business model reengineering" to survive in this new world.

(vii) Automation breakthroughs will see more and more everyday tasks done by machines.

(viii) Cost structures in the Cloud will enable more radical and global low-cost solutions.

(ix)   Widening of the "great divide" between those with digital access and those without.

(x)   The need for the workforce to reskill.

2020 is not that far away. The pace of change is such that what's in the lab today can quickly become the killer app of tomorrow. The iPhone and iPad show just what can happen if a company can get the user interface right. Apple hit the magic button with those new products. They have shown, very clearly, what it takes to succeed. And the answer is simple: you need the software breakthrough plus – and it's a big plus – you need to make it fascinating and amazing to interact with it. A great example is the Gesture Cube, where interactive 3D steps out of the movie and becomes real!

All corporations are now at a cross-roads. They can either examine their future and embrace the new digital world. Or they can keep their head down and hope that its real impact will be delayed. For many their future "strategy" is still only looking out for at most 12 months. The excuse is: How can we look out any further when the world is changing so rapidly? This short-termism allows execs to develop an incremental holding path where a mix of cost-cutting and fighting to maintain customer contracts might just about deliver some kind of acceptable budget plan. And after all, there's always the credit crunch to blame and its dampening effect on consumer spending and business investment.

But eventually this type of "strategy" is just not going to work. Eventually the new players and rivals will reach critical mass with their new software and approaches. Eventually consumer behavior will change to such a degree that for example a big retailer just will not need all that space to merchandize and display products when it's all available more conveniently online. That may happen in 3 years or 5 but the impact of this technology revolution will be felt; it will not go away or lessen. And so that crossroads is here. And companies need to decide what to do about it.

Kodak is one example we'll review later. Their crossroads has already come. Their crisis arrived much quicker than expected. The company had tried the incremental survive-the-next-12-months approach, but they did not get away with it. Their "moment of truth" came early. The good news is that their leadership embarked on what will be a 10-year transformation journey ... a journey that is taking them from a 20th century dinosaur to potentially a 21st century winner. Which other companies can genuinely claim to be on that journey? Who is going to be the next big corporate to crash through short-term myopic planning? And which ones are going to be the next generation winners we should be watching and investing in?

2 Our Lives Are About to Change Forever

Our lives are about to change forever. It's starting to impact every company, every organization and most every one of us on this planet. It's a totally transforming and headline-grabbing era that we are privileged to be witnessing. It ranks alongside the other major challenges of our day like global-warming and our care for the environment, scarcity of resources such as oil and water and the growing divide between rich and poor. It's one of the keys that will shape and define this first part of the 21st century.

This book is all about the extremely rapid development of digital technology, the internet and mobile communication. There is without doubt a technology revolution unfolding that's as life-changing as the invention of the wheel. Its importance is highlighted because it touches all of us every day and in every way. We perhaps don't see the eureka moments, we maybe don't realize the seismic shifts, but they are happening. By 2020 we will see a fundamentally different world. What was once an idea is fast becoming the new reality.

Every part of every day we find ourselves propelled headlong into the world of digital technology and interaction. Our clock, radio, phone, TV and most every gadget we wake up to is digital. Our news feeds might come from satellite or by RSS feed to our favorite website or our own news portal. Our bus/train journey to work is interrupted or enriched by iTunes or by last night's TV or the day's papers on our iPad or Notebook. Our time at work is driven around computer and mobile. We are slaves to email at our desk, away from our desk with our Blackberry or smart phone. We are dependent upon Google to find things out. Meetings get scheduled for us on Outlook, the direct-dial landline phone on our desk remains silent and unused. Our IT department is constantly in demand to fix this laptop, download this application, resync my phone and my online. We do our own PowerPoint presentations, we don't have any assistant and the pressure is on the individual to master the technology and be able to use it. And for time after work, we are connected via Facebook, tweeting on Twitter, using location-based services to find the best local bars and pubs. And we are completely, totally reliant on this technology. We just assume it will work, just as we trust our alarm clock to wake us up in the morning. It's the wheel that turns our lives.

And all this is being master-minded by just a few multi-national organizations. They already are dominating and their influence is going to grow.

▷ Google own YouTube. They also own DoubleClick, AdMob and a host of other general and niche market-leading businesses. They vigorously promote Google Chrome web browser as an alternative to Internet Explorer, Android (the mobile phone operating system), Earth and Maps, Google TV and many other truly innovative applications.

▷ Microsoft has a 1.6% share of Facebook and a small shareholding (albeit <5%) in Apple. In 2011 it announced a major global strategic alliance with Nokia which was expected to lead to its takeover of that company. It has acquired Skype for a mind-boggling $8bn even though Skype is still loss-making. What Skype does give Microsoft is access to its 600 million users and community and control of the world's largest international voice and video call company. It has also acquired more than 150 other companies or strategic stakes in the past 20 years.

These companies together have huge cash war chests. Microsoft still had some $35bn at time of writing, Apple had c. $25bn and Google had some $25bn too. And other Tech companies like IBM, Cisco, Intel, HP and Amazon are all cash rich. In fact, the top 12 Tech companies listed in the US have a staggering $215bn of cash searching for investment opportunities. They are among the most valued on the planet (Figure 1).

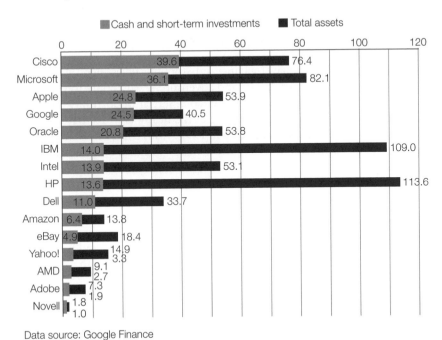

Data source: Google Finance

Figure 1 **Big tech company assets (in billions of USD)**
Source: www.pingdom.com

These are the companies that are changing our lives. These are the ones that are leading the biggest revolution in history. These are the ones that are set to continue to lead the transformation of the global economy and the way human beings interact and communicate. Even as we read this book, history is being made.

It is the speed of this change and the amount of it that is startling. Just at the start of this century, the internet was a "new thing". Boardrooms across the world debated it casually and mostly chose to ignore it. Or, at their most adventurous, they sanctioned a $50k project to "explore all this stuff a bit further".

I can remember the board-room debates in 1999 and 2000 when I headed up Argos.co.uk. At that time Argos was the main retail arm of FTSE 100 company GUS plc. We had just successfully launched "Click 'n Collect" and "Ring 'n Reserve". Internet commentators were seeing Argos as a leading "clicks 'n bricks" company, a leading organization with a proven format and business model for this new "multi-channel age"!

But GUS plc held the purse strings – they decided what to invest, how much and where, and they were not at all convinced by this "internet thing". At the time online sales were about 0.1% of Argos' total revenues. And the GUS board felt that online sales would surely, never, amount to more than 1% of the total. "It's just a fad; it's a passing thing … not worth substantial investment."

And yet, 10 years later and yes, you've guessed it: Argos online was now up to around 40% of the total retail revenues, more than £1.5bn, and expected to continue to grow. Forecasts show it could be as much as 50% by 2014.

And while GUS were navel-gazing and stopping investment at Argos, a number of pioneers and evangelists and adventurers, who could foresee what would happen, started building out the commercial opportunity. Some of course made a lot of money very quickly in the heady Web 1.0 days.

Roger Barnett founded Beauty.com in 1999. Just 12 months later and with revenues standing at around $150k, he sold the business to Drugstore.com for a reported $40m.

Bill Nguyen sold Onebox.com, a small internet messaging business for $850m. Founded in 1998 with all the hype: "the next-generation consumer communications company", just two years later the business was acquired by Phone.com.

StreetsOnline had revenues of around £10m selling CDs and it was loss-making. It was being offered for sale at the height of boom with all kinds of market-backed forecasts and valuations by Morgan Stanley for £750m.

Not surprisingly, as we all know, the bubble burst and there were equally many casualties such as Boo.com, WebVan, Pets.com, eToys, Disney's Go.com and in total some 835 others. But that internet bubble bursting did not stop the continued interest among consumers and business customers for the ease and convenience of web-based information-gathering and transaction processing.

3 How are Consumers and Businesses Responding?

While some industry leaders may have had their doubts – and there are still people who are skeptical about the full potential of the digital world – nevertheless pioneers continued to innovate and, most crucially, demand continued to grow.

▷ B2C e-commerce spending has continued to grow all over the world. From relatively low levels at the start of 2000 (c.f. Argos' 0.1%!), the amount spent by consumers has rocketed to around $300bn in 2010, up 800% (eMarketer and US Census stats).

▷ Forecast annual growth rates globally for online retail over the 5 years from 2011 vary from 8% to 13% per year compound, with markets in Asia "set to explode" (IMRG and Forrester).

▷ In the meantime B2B commerce (which includes pure online B2B trades as well software sales to automate or facilitate online transaction activity) has soared to $3.7 trillion, with around half of this coming from the Americas (US Census/eMarketer).

▷ The number of internet-hosted domain names has risen to nearly 800 million (Internet Systems Consortium).

▷ Online advertising spend has grown globally. In the US spend is now up to c.$24bn in just 10 years and, while all ad spend suffered a dip in the 2008/09 recession and credit crunch, it has picked right back up in 2011 (Figure 2).

▷ Online ad spend is replacing traditional media such as press, radio and TV. For example, in the UK it is now the largest total media spend channel (PWC/IAB).

▷ In 1995, the web reached about 5% of the US population and on average they spent around 30 minutes per day online. In 2010/11, the web reached c. 75% of the US population and average time spent online per user per day was more than 2 hours (Ball State University Centre for Media Studies).

▷ Looking at this another way, internet penetration has grown from c. 200 million households worldwide in 2000 to an estimated 1.8 billion in 2010/11 (Digital Advertising).

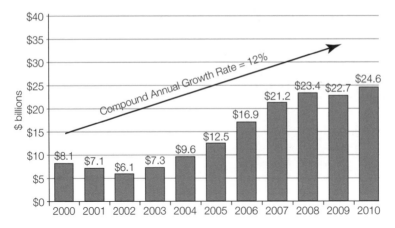

Figure 2   **Spending on interactive advertising**
Source: Interactive Advertising Bureau.

▷ Facebook.com has some 600 million+ users worldwide at the time of writing. On average, 50% of them log on every day. An average user has 130 friends. People spend 700 billion minutes a month on Facebook. The site is available in 70 different languages and is accessed in more than 60 countries. 200 million active users engage via their mobile phone (source: Facebook). The population of Facebook would make it the third largest country in the world. In 2011, Facebook announced they were targeting one billion registered users.

And we can go on … there are countless stats to show how quickly all this has been happening, how it is displacing traditional ways of doing business, communicating and interacting, how it is affecting everything we do. Here's a selection of some recent headlines and case studies describing how digital has specifically changed someone's life or an organization's or region's prospects:

▷ Guardian Media Group transformed its fortunes. AutoTrader used to be a regular consumer print magazine showing classified ads for cars, vans, trucks etc. In 2002, Autotrader.co.uk was launched and has rapidly grown. It now has 10 million visitors per month, while the hard copy magazine continues to decline in sales and circulation. It has more recently launched a site for use on mobile phones which has attracted an incremental 500,000 monthly visitors. It's now valued at $3bn.

▷ Network operators are transforming communications in Shanghai. They are developing 'triple play' pilots which combine telephone, internet and interactive TV into a 'next generation fourth network'. This will impact 2.5 million downtown users in the first wave.

▷ Eastman Kodak has transformed itself, and the change to digital technology is providing a real chance of recovery. CEO Antonio Perez is credited with leading this corporate revolution. In 2010/11, 75% of Kodak's business and 60% of profits will come from digital services. In 2003, Kodak was at its most vulnerable as its main film business, which up till then had contributed some 90% of revenues and 100% of the profits, went into accelerated decline. Perez came in and immediately cut costs, closed down film production and distribution operations. He then started to restructure the assets and made a series of acquisitions to transform the company into a 'digital imaging' business. There are now two core divisions: Consumer, which provides digital cameras, photo frames and video; and Commercial Graphics, which provides scanning, pre-press, digital plate-making and related workflow software and digital printing.

Kodak invented the first film camera and the first digital camera, now after 7 years of tough transformation the new digital Kodak has basically been formed. This transformation is expected to be complete by 2014. Kodak needed to build a new culture of digital technology while not losing sight of their core values and imaging heritage. Their experience and lessons learned during this transformation can be applied to any company in any industry. Kodak had to go back to basics in many areas in order to redefine their core skills and services and what would create value to customers.

2010 revenues for the new divisions grew 15% and they were expecting continued and even stronger growth. The consumer inkjet business, for example, continues to outpace the market and they are on track to double their ink revenue. Demand has been driven by Kodak's hybrid digital printing systems and processes which help customers to capitalize on new business opportunities. Kodak will continue to focus on product innovation and maximize the value of their IP. Net cash generation before the ongoing restructuring costs was more than $400m. The journey is far from complete and Kodak's markets are highly competitive but they do now have a clear strategy, vision and plan for where they want to get to.

▷ "It's true, moms: Tech can spell salvation. Plenty of moms out there may not think of themselves as extraordinarily tech-savvy, [but] technology is probably affecting your daily life ... in more ways than you may realize."

Laura Coffey, writing on today.msnbc.msn.com, explained as follows:

1   Using a smart phone means mums can keep in touch both by phone and email, use the map function to get directions to the next children's party, take photos of those cute occasions and in moments of desperation bring tantrums to a halt by launching a fun kids video or playing some music, and all on one device which is easy to use and less likely to get lost.

2   Using the Eye-Fi camera memory card automatically downloads photos to a computer via a Wi-Fi connection. Even if the computer is

turned off, photos and video clips can still be uploaded to any photo-sharing site such as Flickr or Kodak Gallery. No more messing about with USB cable plugs or trying to find time to do those file transfers. All now done automatically!

3   Flylady.net is a great site to help busy mums stay in control of their lives! It's full of encouraging and supportive tips and puts women more in touch with whole networks of other mums for advice, support, ideas and just to chat.

4   Sites like WebMD, iVillage and Yahoo! Parenting all give lots of instant guidance and medical advice.

5   And finally, Facebook lets mums quickly and easily stay in touch with all their friends!

▷ Here's a profile of a typical 10 year old. Let's call him Alexander. He spends his spare time on Nintendo DS or on X-Box Kinect, does school homework research on Google, prepares Word and PowerPoint docs and presentations for class work, has his own PC and wants an Apple Mac, is the class ICT Monitor to check everyone gets good web access, has a "pay-as-you-go" mobile phone and is in regular texting and Skype contact with his grandma and cousins, is adept at using his mum's iPhone and is now asked to find directions on Google maps if they're driving somewhere new in the car, has his own iPod and already has downloaded some 250 tunes, plugs in earphones and is away in his music collection, wants an iTouch, is uploading photos of his latest Lego builds to Lego club and getting Dad to email them to ask why the photos aren't yet included in the Lego magazine and wants more Lego for Xmas (yes, the actual physical bricks, somewhat surprisingly given everything else is digital!). And Alexander laughs when his parents explain that when they were kids they didn't have a color TV!!

▷ In 2002, Rupert Murdoch, Chairman and CEO of News Corp, published a best-selling biographical account: *The Murdoch Mission: the digital transformation of a media empire*. The book charts the early insight as to how technology would start to fundamentally change the way consumers and business access news and content. News Corp is now the world's third largest media conglomerate behind only Disney and Time Warner. Not bad for a company that started out in the 1970s owning a small group of newspapers in Australia.

Murdoch realized two key things: (i) unique and original content would be 'king' and would always command a price in the market place and (ii) that people's media consumption habits would change as the internet grew and technology advanced.

Murdoch has taken a stream of initiatives to embrace new technology. Most notably, he led the hard-fought and strike-ridden changeover at the Times Newspaper's old printing presses in Wapping, east London, to adopt new technologies, automate processes, allow flexible working practices and reduce costs.

His greatest push over the past 5 years, as noted in a Wiki collaboration, has been into digital assets. Not just in the way that News Corp across all its divisions now creates, distributes and archives around consolidated digital hubs which feed all channels of distribution, but also in the way that he has invested in and acquired other businesses which were already established, brought in related skills and know-how and provided News Corp with a firm foothold in the digital media landscape:

Summary of News Corp's Internet/Digital Assets

▶ *Fox Interactive Media*
  ▷ Foxsports.com – website with sports news, scores, statistics, video and fantasy sports and on MSN.
  ▷ MySpace Video, now owned by Specific Media and Justin Timberlake, hosts content from the Net and studios, competes with Google's YouTube.
  ▷ Beliefnet – largest online faith and spirituality network.
  ▷ Hulu (27%) – online video streaming site in partnership with NBC Universal and Walt Disney.
  ▷ Flektor – provides web-based tools for photo and video editing and mashups.
  ▷ IGN Entertainment – internet entertainment portal (includes the sites IGN, GameSpy, TeamXbox, and Askmen.com)
  ▷ Giga.de
  ▷ Slingshot Labs – web development incubator (includes the site DailyFill).
  ▷ Strategic Data Corp – interactive advertising company which develops technology to deliver targeted internet advertising.
  ▷ Scout.com.
  ▷ WhatIfSports.com – sports simulation and prediction website. Also provides fantasy-style sports games to play.
▶ *Indya.com – 'India's no. 1 Entertainment Portal'.*
▶ *News Digital Media*
  ▷ News.com.au – Australian-oriented news website
    ▶ News Lab
  ▷ CareerOne.com.au (50%) – recruitment advertisement website in partnership with Monster Worldwide.
  ▷ Carsguide.com.au
  ▷ in2mobi.com.au
  ▷ TrueLocal.com.au
  ▷ Moshtix.com.au – A ticket retailer
  ▷ Learning Seat
  ▷ Wego News owns minority stake in Wego.com
  ▷ Netus (75%) – investment co. in online properties.
▶ *REA Group (60.7%)*
  ▷ Realestate.com.au
  ▷ Casa.it (69.4%), Sky Italia also holds a 30.6% share
  ▷ atHome group, operator of leading real estate websites in Luxembourg, France, Belgium and Germany.
    ▶ Altowin (51%), provider of office management tools for real estate agents in Belgium.
  ▷ Propertyfinder.com (50%), News International holds the remaining 50%
    ▶ Sherlock Publications, owner of hotproperty.co.uk portal and magazine titles 'Hot Property', 'Renting' and 'Overseas'
    ▶ ukpropertyshop.co.uk, most comprehensive UK estate agent directory.
  ▷ PropertyLook, property websites in Australia and New Zealand.
  ▷ HomeSite.com.au, home renovation and improvement website.
  ▷ Square Foot Limited, Hong Kong's largest English Language property magazine and website.
    ▶ Primedia – Holding co. of Inside DB, a Hong Kong lifestyle magazine.
▶ *TadpoleNetMedia (10%) hosts ArmySailor*
▶ *New Zealand*
  ▷ DVD Unlimited – leading online DVD subscription service (ownership through stake in Sky Network Television).
  ▷ Fox Networks – one of the largest international ad networks.
  ▷ Expedient InfoMedia blog network.
▶ *UK*
  ▷ Times Newspaper group
  ▷ BSkyB strategic shareholding

Recently, Rupert Murdoch has decided to take on the Education sector which has generally been making a slow transition from textbook to online learning. Leading companies were surprised when News Corp announced its acquisition at end of 2010/11 of New York-based education technology company Wireless Generation for $360m. Wireless Generation uses mobile devices, assessment software and databases to help teachers track student performance and tailor individual instruction.

News Corp see the Education sector as one that has not yet been transformed by digital technology and estimate that just 15% of the US education market, worth around $28bn in annual revenues, comes from digital sources. According to a leading education analyst, "technology spending [is] still growing in spite of tight state budgets because of mounting evidence that it can improve student's results." (The Financial Times Limited, 2011)

And yet, despite the headlines, despite the way digital is very starkly changing our lives and radically impacting the way business must interact with its customers, still many corporations have yet to fully grasp this new world of opportunity. Even though traditional business models may be under threat, especially in the Media and Retail industry and with other sectors not far behind, yet many cling on to the same ways of doing things. Sure they may make some "digital investments" so they can appease stock market analysts, reassuring them that they are "forward-thinking" and not got their heads buried in the sand. But many are kind of hoping that this digital revolution won't quite affect them yet. They plan so that potentially they can just about squeeze out another year or two of earnings growth from the current business model (perhaps primarily through cost-cutting) and if they can, then they can move on and leave the really difficult digital transformation to their successors.

Many executive team leaders are quick to acknowledge that the digital revolution is here to stay and that in the future they will often have to fundamentally adapt and innovate their existing business model. But the process of change, especially transformational change, is very hard to accomplish. And so most postpone that day.

But for just how long will it be justifiable to make that postponement? How long can executive teams delay the inevitable? How long before a company's own shareholders start demanding urgent action? How long will it take before every business realizes it must go through radical change if it is to become one of the winning businesses of tomorrow? Only those that do grasp the nettle will have a chance of survival. And the sooner they start on the journey the better. After all, it has taken Kodak seven years to rebuild its business and they see at least a further three years to go!

4 The World in 2020

At the start of this decade our digital world was largely based on "Point and Click". It's what we still do. We're still largely chained to our desk with our PC. We move a cursor across the screen and click. Websites are built that way and e-commerce is driven that way. User journeys are written that way and web analysis and metrics are managed that way. We're contained within a small rectangular box with a standard screen resolution of fixed pixel-array display of typically 1024×768 (though we also now see 1440×900 as screens get bigger). We live with tool bars across the top and often bottom of the screen taking up to 25% of the space. That's how web pages are designed. It's how we think about the computer and it governs the principal way we use digital technology and how we interact.

But inevitably and inexorably we are starting to move away from this constraining form of interface and interaction. And the breakthrough really has been touch technology. Invented as far back as 1971 by Dr Sam Hurst while at the University of Kentucky, it then took a number of years to move out of the lab and into the real commercial world. Citibank became the pioneers. In 1986, they ripped out their old button and keypad ATMs in New York and Hong Kong and replaced them with a simple touch screen user interface. That move had the same market place impact then as the iPhone has had more recently. It was revolutionary and innovative and changed the way enterprising businesses thought about new product development. Not long after, we started seeing touch screen kiosks in-store. The first nationwide interactive kiosks were found in the Florsheim shoe store chain across the US. They were basic and at that time lacked any internet connectivity but they were product information focused and, because they were new and had a novelty value, they attracted plenty of interest. Apple themselves were already very active in exploring this area and they launched the forerunner of the iPhone/iPad in 1993 with their Apple Newton. (An alternative but similar device was the Palm Pilot and these two devices between them dominated the handheld market sector at the time.)

The Apple Newton was not intended to be a computer but a "personal digital assistant" or PDA (a term coined by Apple's then CEO John Sculley who was a key creator of Apple as we know it today). It used touch screen and stylus pen, enabling users to manage information such as Notes, Calendar, Contacts, Schedules etc. The built-in handwriting recognition was one of its major new features and attracted a lot of interest, developing ideas about subsequent computer interaction which need not only be driven by

Source: Apple Inc.

mouse and keyboard. But the Newton and Pilot were bulky (over an inch thick), heavy (weighing about one pound) and, of course, at that time in the mid-1990s they had no wireless internet capability, although they could be connected via cable to the PC to at least sync up data.

All these developments were preparing the ground for the iPhone, iPod, iTouch and iPad which have now made touch screen technology widely available, exciting to use and quickly becoming the default user interface.

So we're starting to move away from a world of "Point and Click". We're arriving at the next stage on the journey. It's now about simple "Touch and Go!"

The "old", desk-based and wired computer environment we've grown up with is starting to look distinctly dinosaur-like! It's as though computing has been in a dark and primitive phase. Our desks have been covered with cables. We've been surrounded by boxes and routers and modems. We've been living in an electronic spaghetti junction. If we've wanted to take advantage of digital technology we've had to become experts in configuring ports, formatting drives, understanding our server SMTP spec, wrestling with ISPs, worrying about RAM capacity, negotiating data caps on broadband subscriptions ... The logistics of operating and interacting in the digital world have been complex, deterred many and certainly slowed down rates of uptake and adoption.

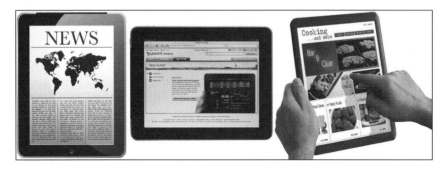

So the iPad has been well received because it starts us on the road to where all these roadblocks are a thing of the past. Here's a potential dream machine that can combine all the major computing and communication functions in one convergent device. It's portable. It's wireless. It's glossy and sleek and feels good. It's very responsive and intuitive. It connects with us directly and intimately. It works and will mark an historical shift in computing and digital interaction.

But this is just the start of the next phase in the era of computing and human interaction. It's only a matter of time before Speech Recognition software reaches such a level of reliability and accuracy that it will become more widely incorporated in our everyday computer interaction. Although the first "speech recogniser" was developed in 1964 and exhibited by IBM, it took another 30 years of lab work before it was ready to be considered for a full commercial roll-out. Microsoft were the unsung pioneers here, and they developed their own speech recognition technology which was first made widely available in Office 2003. It has since evolved so that it is embedded in all Microsoft Windows and Office products. Apple Macs have been slower to adopt this functionality but they now have their own award-winning product called Dictate.

What does this Microsoft and Apple software do? There are two core functions: Dictate, turning speech into text, and Command – speak and the computer will respond. The Microsoft and Apple software tools have their rivals. Dedicated speech recognition software providers like e-Speaking, TalkingDesktop and TalktoyourComputer all offer a variety of features such as voice commands already built-in and ready to activate, e.g. Open Email, File Open, Select, Next Page. Such is the competition that these software tools are available on free trials and download with low subsequent one-off license or monthly payments. There are also specialist tools, for example, for the medical/health care professions so that more arcane vocabulary is easily and quickly recognized.

The suppliers claim around 90% accuracy, with further improvements as the computer gets used to your voice. What's more, the computer is now also being given its own voice to speak back. For the present that is restricted to responses like "File is Opened", "Job is Complete". But this "computer response ability" is very much at an early stage of development and is not yet at an interactive level. The next stage is Computer Prompt. This is a function by which the computer will talk to you: "New Email" is an obvious one, but that is evolving to calendar/meeting alerts: "Your next meeting is in 30 minutes." And as devices converge we could expect to hear, for example, "You have a call waiting from your partner, shall I put it through?" or "Hurry up, you're late for your next meeting!" Is this just a few steps away from the computer HAL in the avant-garde Kubrick movie *2001* in which HAL is able to act independently? And while that is a stimulating idea, such an invention is (sadly?) without doubt outside the 2020 timeframe of this book. (Even the most gung-ho futurologists I have spoken to agree that genuine artificial intelligence is beyond this decade.)

But why is the voice recognition trend critical? Just as the iPad has innovated around touch and has tapped into that very intimate set of tactile and intuitive response mechanisms, so devices are being developed that can truly integrate and harness the ability of speech as well. It means that we can now start to enter a digital world which is much closer to "Touch and Talk."

It's exciting because it is now much more about the computer being "wired" into our brain, rather than into the router. It taps more deeply into a wider range of our core senses. All of a sudden instead of it all just being about what you can see, the whole experience becomes much more immersive and engaging. We are connecting with much more of our core being.

It's now about Sight and Sound and Touch and Talk. Our bodily senses are being connected, not just our brains. And that's why devices that can exploit this are so successful. Only Smell and Taste remain completely elusive, for the time-being…

So we are moving away from Point and Click. We are firmly into an era of "Touch and Go!". It is only a matter of time before further voice integration takes us into "Touch and Talk". But is that the end of the journey?

Not surprisingly, the answer is that over the decade to 2020 the next evolution is already waiting in the wings. Early prototypes are out of the lab and are available to buy. They may still be a bit clunky but they are the next stage of our future and the next step in digital technology development.

Gesture Cube is the latest innovation that points the way to yet a further stage of progress. It uses electric field sensing technology to make 3D spatial hand or finger movement tracking possible. It also employs proximity detection technology. It provides a 3D interactive experience. It detects your hand's approach and movement and responds to your gestures. You just wave your hand to control the device! These natural hand movements interact with a computing device to become the means of navigation, image and content movement and selection. The hand gestures are intuitive and effortless and can indeed feel magical.

Gest-Cube 3D technology is currently being featured on a new product from Indent Technology (based in Germany) working in partnership with design engineers at Lunar, who are based in Palo Alto.

This product is currently being marketed as a home entertainment device (Plate 1 in the center of the book). Wave your hand, navigate and choose. Select what music you want to listen to, what photos or videos to share and in what order, what movies to watch. But the technology itself works outside of this Gesture Cube product. It could, for example, enable 3D hand control on 2D screens so it could work on a smart phone or tablet PCs, picture frames and iPads.

Another initiative in this arena which is already widespread is the Xbox Kinect. This uses different technology but looks to achieve a similar end result, allowing remote unconnected hand movement to control what takes place on screen. Kinect relies on range camera technology developed by the Israeli company Prime Sense. This in effect determines 3D scene information from a continuously projected infra-red structured light. The Kinect camera and software provide full body 3D motion capture as well as facial and voice recognition capabilities. Kinect can track up to two active players for motion analysis and can track 20 joint movements at any one time.

Kinect is similar to Gesture Cube in that it is utilizing software to track remote movement, and the camera technology gives an extended practical range of about 3 meters. And while, of course, current developments at Xbox are focused on gaming and new game experiences, Kinect has also served the purposes of bringing hand controlled remote wireless 3D interaction into the mass market and moving consumer expectations and acceptance along another notch.

It means we're getting ever closer to a world which was first showcased in the Tom Cruise film *Minority Report*. This was a Stephen Spielberg directed movie which came out in 2002 (based on a short story by Philip K. Dick). Spielberg wanted to present a plausible future world and is said to have consulted with a number of scientists and technologists to provide a realistic and authentic future scenario. Fifteen experts convened at a now famous 3-day "think tank" session. These included architect Peter Calthorpe, author Douglas Coupland, computer scientist Neil Gershenfeld, biomedical researcher Shaun Jones, computer scientist Jaron Lanier, and former Massachusetts Institute of Technology (MIT) technology architecture dean William J. Mitchell. So there was some real in-depth thought and input that was being captured.

What was so innovative and exciting about this movie and why did its "sci-fi realism" strike such a chord? It was simply because you could sense that the technology was in reach. Even though the technology did not exist in 2002, nevertheless people could see how likely it could be and could believe in this future world. What is extraordinary is that 10 years later a lot of the ideas in the movie are fast becoming reality.

The most powerful visual idea in the movie was the way in which Cruise interacted with computer-generated imagery. He was able to tell the computer to bring up a 3D holographic display of various screen pages and images from a computer memory bank. He could interact with that imagery using voice commands or by touch. Just as we do with an iPad today, he could stretch, shift, zoom, extend, move to the "next page" with a simple touch or with what could become a Gest-Cube-like hand wave. It was as though he was interacting seamlessly and completely with 3D and holographic displays. There was no sense of there even being pages from a computer – it was just content and material which could be summoned, moved and sorted. Cruise's manipulation of content and imagery was presented in the film as if he were conducting an orchestra. But this was an orchestra of content, not just people. They called it the "spatial operating environment interface".

News and information sources from Wikipedia and elsewhere have noted that the future technologies depicted in the film were prescient. The *Guardian* published a piece titled "Why *Minority Report* was spot on" in June 2010. And the following month Fast Company examined seven crime-fighting technologies in the film that were similar to ones that were actually becoming available. National Public Radio in the US published an August 2010 podcast which also analyzed the film's accuracy in predicting future technologies. One of the big ideas in the film was said by Hewlett-Packard to have been a major motivator to conduct further research – in HP's case to develop cloud computing.

Technologies from the film that were later realized include:

▷ *Multi-touch interfaces* put out by Obscura (2008), MIT (2009), Intel (2009), and Microsoft for their Xbox 360 (2010). A company representative, at the 2007 premiere of the Microsoft Surface, promised it "will feel like *Minority Report*". When Microsoft released the Kinect motion-sensing camera add-on for their Xbox 360 gaming console in 2010, the Kinect's technology allowed several programmers, including students at MIT, to create what they called "*Minority Report* inspired user interfaces".

▷ *Retina scanners*, developed by a Manhattan company named Global Rain-makers Incorporated (GRI) (2010). The company is installing hundreds of the scanners in Bank of America locations and has a contract to install them on several United States Air Force bases.

▷ *Insect robots*, similar to the film's spider robots, developed by the US Military. These insects will be capable of reconnoiter missions in dangerous areas not fit for soldiers, such as "occupied houses". They serve the same purpose in the film. According to the developer, BAE Systems, the "goal is to develop technologies that will give our soldiers another set of eyes and ears for use in urban environments and complex terrain, places where they cannot go or where it would be too dangerous."

▷ *Facial recognition advertising billboards*, being developed by the Japanese company NEC. These billboards will theoretically be able to recognize passers-by via facial recognition, call them by name, and deliver customer-specific advertisements. Thus far the billboards can recognize age and gender, and deliver demographically appropriate adverts, but cannot discern individuals. According to *The Daily Telegraph*, the billboards will "behave like those in ... *Minority Report* ... in which Cruise's character is confronted with digital signs that call out his name as he walks through a futuristic shopping mall." IBM is developing similar billboards which plan to deliver customized adverts to individuals who carry identity tags. Like NEC, the company feels they will not be obtrusive as their billboards will only advertize products which a customer is interested in. Advertisers are keen to embrace these types of personalized promotion as they figure to reduce costs by lowering the number of adverts wasted on uninterested consumers.

▷ *Electronic paper*, developments announced by Xerox (2002), MIT (2005), media conglomerate Hearst Corporation (2008), and LG the electronics manufacturer (2010). Xerox has been trying to develop something similar to e-paper since before the film was released. In 2005, when the *Washington Post* asked the chief executive of the MIT spin-off handling their research when "the '*Minority Report*' newspaper" would be released, he predicted "around 2015." TechWatch's 2008 article, "'*Minority Report*' e-newspaper on the way", noted that Hearst was "pushing large amounts of cash" into the technology. In discussing the LG announcement, Cnet commented that "if you thought electronic newspapers were the stuff of science fiction, you're quite right. They first featured in the film *Minority Report*, released in 2002."

So all this starts to bring color and life to our future world – a world that is very much just around the corner. In less than 10 years much of Spielberg's vision is fast becoming reality. The old dinosaur days of "point and click" will soon become a distant memory. We are moving through Touch and Go!

to "Touch and Talk", and we are beginning to see signs of a Cruise-type/ Gest-Cube/3D interactive-type world that can be described as "Command and Connect".

And, as if this is not enough, we also have developments around "brain-driven" computer control where implants in the brain can be used to order and control the computer screen. We are at the early stages of controlling computers just by thinking. Thought control has had especial early application for people who are paralyzed. An article in *Nature* magazine shows how someone who is paralyzed from the neck down can nevertheless control a computer, play games, change channels on TV, and manipulate a robot just by thinking: "Think and Move!" This brain-to-machine connection is getting ever closer and has relied principally on implanting electrodes to respond to the electrical activity associated with certain movements. An alternative method being trialled places electrodes on the scalp and the computer learns to associate particular brain signals with intended actions. CeBIT 2010 saw the launch of the world's first patient-ready commercially available brain computer interface. And there are many companies experimenting with such devices. The cap that sits on the scalp to capture the brain's electrical signals is becoming more user-friendly and easier to wear. It's assumed that eventually no cap will be needed and the computer will be controllable by thoughts alone. In the same way that a computer can recognize a voice, it can also be "taught", it's believed, to remotely scan and pick up the brain's electrical impulses. (The Emotiv wearable headset, pictured in Plate 2 in the center of the book, demonstrates that what was once functional and ugly has started to become useable.)

In fact, according to announcements from Intel in 2009, "chips in brains will control computers by 2020". Researchers at Intel have concluded that it will only be a matter of time before we see the end of the keyboard and the mouse and surf the Net using just our brain waves. The brain would be enhanced by Intel-developed sensors that are implanted. Experiments are currently taking place with robots and there are already examples of manipulating a robot using the brain of a monkey! It may sound far-fetched but the Intel research prediction of a 2020 deadline is serious. And this leads us on inevitably and inexorably to one of the ultimate medium-term goals of developing genuine artificial intelligence. There are many research teams across the globe looking at how to integrate software in order to enhance the processing speed and power of the human brain and to potentially add new knowledge immediately via a plug 'n play routine!

Significant effort is currently being devoted to making human interaction with computers and with information in general more simple, natural and seamless. "The pace of advances in computing, communication, mobile, robotic, and interactive technologies is accelerating," Ahmed Noor points out in a recent review in *Mechanical Engineering*. "The trend towards digital convergence of these technologies with information technology, virtual worlds, knowledge-based engineering and artificial intelligence is ushering in a new era."

And Noor goes on to predict "ecosystems [that] will be populated by a dynamic aggregation of humans, cognitive robots, virtual world platforms and other digital components ... Humans will have multisensory, immersive 3-D experience in mixed physical-virtual worlds..." The emphasis in this future world – Cloud 2.0-based? – will be on optimizing human performance.

The human experience of the computer to date has been for us to immerse ourselves in it; we have had to learn to work in the computer's world of scroll bars, list controls, mouse and keyboard. But we don't live there. Even with the iPhone we are still interacting with the device on its terms in its world. But, we exist in our own three-dimensional world. And what will start to happen is that the computer will increasingly come to us. It will start to recognize who is sitting in front of it or who is holding it. It will recognize our voice and react when we talk to it. Breakthroughs such as the Xbox Kinect and Gest-Cube show that the computer can learn to react to *our* physical movements and the advances in BCI (brain computer interaction) demonstrate further how we will be able to exert control, on our terms and in ways that suit us, not chained to the desktop!

Here's one vision of the future from Sam Martin speaking at a *Forbes* magazine conference about our world in 2020:

> In the future nearly every visible thing will be catalogued and indexed, ready to be instantly identifiable and described to us. Want to go shopping? In the future we won't need big retail stores with aisles of objects on display. We'll be able to shop out in the [virtual] world ... Do you like that new car you saw drive by? Or those cool shoes on the woman sitting across the room? All you'll have to do is look at it and your mobile handset or AR-equipped [augmented reality-equipped] eye-glasses will identify the object and look up the best price and retailer.

And with the voice command "Buy it," it's your's! The virtual shopping scenario shown in Plate 3 in the center of the book may not be so far in the future.

This future is all going to be about the way that humans can interact with computers. Digital technology will be everywhere, everything will be reducible to digital data, and will have been recorded and therefore become accessible. Instead of sitting in front of a PC or holding a tablet, computers will be built into everything around us and interaction will happen naturally. They will become "invisible tools which will blend into everyday life".

The next generation may never see a computer screen in the physical and formal way that has been used up till now. They will summon content and information on the go wherever and whenever they want it, they will organize and select from it in whichever way they want, they will send it to friends/colleagues by simple voice command or hand wave. As a result you won't even need to carry a mobile phone, instead you'll be able to access Wi-Fi or 4G or other networks and simply say a number or pick it off a called-up content sheet. News can be summoned and read via holographic display or on electronic paper and can be "dismissed" when no longer required. It will be an extraordinary new world and by 2020 we will already be seeing this sort of environment gaining critical mass.

The ongoing evolution of our interaction with technology may be summarized as follows:

Eras of Computing and Human Interaction

1990 to 2009   *Point and Click*

▼

2009 to 2012   *Touch 'n Go!*

▼

2012 to 2015   *Touch 'n Talk*

▼

2015 to 2018   *Command 'n Connect*

▼

2018 to 2020   *Think Talk Move*

---

5 Digital/Multi-channel Checklist

In this new era of digital innovation and adventure, it is now much more challenging for a Brand to engage with its customers. In the "good old days", there were relatively few choices. There were three main channels of engagement and distribution:

▷ Above the line (ATL): a mix of TV (if the brand budget could afford it), typically some press/print and, if feeling bold, a radio ad.
▷ Below the line (BTL): leaflet/sample distribution to people's homes.
▷ In-Store: point of sale incentives and information.

A brand marketing team was used to that set of choices. Agencies were skilled at understanding those specific options and the work load could be divided between two or three agencies: one for the ATL, one for the BTL and one for other stuff! But now, as the 21st century gathers pace, it's all become a lot more complicated. At the last count there were at least 30 different channel and communication options:

Multi-channel options

TV broadcast 30" or interactive, Cinema (3-D or not 3-D?), Radio, Print, Mobile ad or content sponsorship, apps for smart phones, apps for tablets like iPad, pod casts/vod casts, Bluetooth mobile, Direct Marketing, e-mail, catalogue, telemarketing, sales reps, poster, outdoor/event, kiosks, vending, PR, Social Media, Sponsorship, In-game advertising, Point of sale, In-store, on cart, website, online advertising, Search, viral video, affiliates....

It's become a bit of a dinner-party game these days to see if you can identify any others! There is just a bewildering array of choice for any brand marketing team and an almost impossible set of decisions about channel mix, budget allocation, which channels to prioritize and which to ignore. In addition, the audience that a Brand must reach has now become fragmented and widely dispersed, and does not consume media in the easy-to-reach passive way that it used to.

TV, once the home of mass audience reach, is now fragmented and unreliable. It has soared from a few mainstream channels to many hundreds. It's available live or in catch up, via cable or satellite, via internet-connected TV or even down the broadband phone line. People no longer just watch right through a program. They can skip through ad breaks, e.g. on Sky+ or Tivo. They multi-task and might have one eye on the TV set, the other on their Facebook page and also be watching for tweets and emails on Twitter and/or speaking with friends via Skype or instant messaging. Engaging with this audience in the most efficient and effective way has become mesmerizing and complex.

Multi-channel: Key challenges

▷ Which channels deliver the best return on investment (ROI)?
▷ Which campaigns work best on which channels?
▷ If we communicate via channel A then is there a "must-have" complementary channel B that also needs to be involved?
▷ Is there an ideal channel mix?
▷ Can we "afford" to ignore, for example, social media or mobile?
▷ Or can we "afford" to ignore expensive TV and switch to apparently lower-cost online?
▷ Does the channel mix vary by season?
▷ Is there a different channel mix for different target customer segments?
▷ Given that it's all changing so fast and new channel opportunities are emerging, how can we check that what we plan for this year is going to be relevant and appropriate?

The start of an answer to these questions is to best understand what the target customer prefers. But such research can be time-consuming and expensive, it would ideally need to cover all types of segments and audiences and, like a lot of research, may well be inconclusive. So how about an easy top-down approach?

Here's a quick 6 step test to see how far your Brand has already travelled in moving away from traditional media channels and becoming more of a digital multi-channel brand. Each of these steps uses free tools and analysis. They are quick and easy to do.

---

6 Step Test
A brand check for the digital multi-channel age

1 Go to *Adwords.google.com/targeting*. Type in the name of your brand and you will get an instant analysis of monthly traffic, global and local searches as well as any click-through analysis if the brand is being advertised on Google already.

2 Go to *Google.com/insights/search* and you can see the traffic analysis over time – last year, last week – as well as related content/articles that might be influencing those search levels. You can also search at local, country or global level.

3 Now go to *Alexa.com*. You can look up your website and start to get comparative traffic data looking at your brand site versus others in your category. It shows how high the website ranks in terms of traffic generation.

   And amazingly, there is a whole consumer demographic and segmentation analysis that tells you, for example, age, gender, education, family and location.

   Alexa.com will also tell you where your website traffic is coming from so you can work out, for example, if your Brand is Pepsi that the number 1 connecting site in the UK is Sky Sports. That will tell you about existing campaign effectiveness, which ads are working and which are not (for example, the ads on Yahoo may not be working). But it will also start to give you a lot more info on the size and type of your online audience.

   You can begin to start understanding whether and to what degree your Brand is participating in this digital world.

4 Next go to *Facebook.com* and, at the search facility, type in your brand name. You will immediately find the number of Facebook fans and friends you have.

   Again, you can type in competitor brands and see what their numbers are. Is your Brand being left behind in the social media race? Or is this whole category just not of sufficient interest for people to want to talk about it?

   And even more helpfully, you can find out what people are saying about your brand, good and bad. And a similar exercise can be carried out on Twitter.com where the postings and tweets and number of followers can be very immediate and responsive to any marketing or advertising activity.

5 Next, go to *Technorati.com* where, again for free, you can use their Search facility to review the "blogosphere" and find all recent and current blogs about your Brand or any related topic of interest. (www.twingly.com provides a similar search and functionality.)

6 If you want "a one-search-find-all approach", go to *www.socialmention.com* which will trawl through the Net "searching content from across the universe," to quote TalentManagementTech. They will look at all blogs, news, video, audio and images. You can sort by date and by source. It will tell you where comment is coming from and what "buzz words" are generating that comment. But most helpfully, they will also give you a "Sentiment score".

   ▷ The Sentiment score will tell you number of mentions which are positive, negative or neutral.

   ▷ It will also give you an overall sentiment score (ratio of positive to negative comment).

   ▷ There's also a Strength of Sentiment score, which is the percentage likelihood of the brand being discussed in a social media environment.

   ▷ There's a Passion score, which is the percentage likelihood that people talking about your brand will do so repeatedly.

   ▷ Lastly, there's a Reach score which is a range of influence metrics and identifies the number of unique authors referencing the brand divided by the total number of mentions. That will help you to check if it's a few people mentioning you a lot or many with just a casual interest.

   This tool will even give a list of the internet names of the top users/people who talk about this brand and give you a link to them. It's a wonderful way of getting in touch with people who could be or could become key influencers, who may themselves have lots of friends on Facebook and followers on Twitter and themselves can set the tone and reaction to how a product is perceived and rated.

And all this is for free! There are other analytic tools like this, e.g. Sysymos and Filtrbox, which is now owned by Jive Software. Here you can get a free trial but, unlike Social Mention for example, Jive Software have understandably taken a more commercial approach: you are required to sign up for the free trial of Filtrbox and they will then look to convert you into a customer paying for the daily/weekly or monthly "buzz monitoring". Their analysis is presented in a more graphical format so you can also look easily at patterns over time and compare with key competitors. Radian6. com, Steprep.com and Infegy.com provide a similar service.

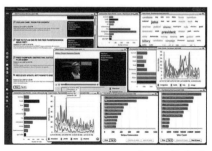

Source: Radian6.

Yet another example, still for free, is Addictomatic. This site enables you to custom build and create your own web page with blocks of content that are regularly updated from Bing news feeds, Google blog search, Facebook, Twitter, YouTube, Flickr, Friendfeed and Wikio.

And there are any number of software companies and brand consultancies offering for a fee to look at these brand monitoring sites and provide a report of what is going on out there in the digital world.

Some Brands have assumed that they are just not relevant enough to generate much social comment. They thought they would be largely untouched by the digital and multi-channel age. But that view can be violently disturbed, especially if something goes wrong. Here's a case study which received such prominence that it became headlines in the *New York*

> ### Key digital brand challenges
> ▷ How digitally engaged is the brand audience?
> ▷ How responsive generally is your product market or sector to a multi-channel approach?
> ▷ Are there any learnings from what competitors are up to?
> ▷ How important are social, mobile and the other multi-channels becoming for short- and medium-term sales and marketing planning?

Times, Huffington Post and countless other media places. It shows how the consumer has become more and more of an influence on brand destiny and that having a "multi-channel" strategy in place is just about essential for any brand, especially one operating in the highly competitive B2C spaces.

When two Domino's Pizza employees filmed a prank in a restaurant's kitchen, they decided to post it online onto YouTube. It showed them messing about with the food. But within just a few days they found themselves on the end of a felony charge. Also, Domino's had more than a million disgusted viewers and faced a public relations crisis. What happened?

Within 48 hours of being posted online, the video had been viewed more than a million times. References to it were in 5 of the 12 results on the first page of a Google search for "Dominos", and discussions about the film had spread throughout Twitter.

As Domino's began to realize, social networking has the reach and speed to turn local incidents into nationwide marketing crises. But they are not alone. Amazon, for example, was forced into an embarrassed apology in the same week for a "ham-fisted" error after Twitter members complained that the sales rankings for gay and lesbian books seemed to have disappeared — and, because Amazon took a few days to respond, the social media world criticized it for being uncommunicative.

Back to Domino's, in just a few days it found its reputation significantly damaged. It became "a nightmare … the toughest situation for a company to face in terms of a digital crisis," in the words of PR consultant, Paul Gallagher. Domino's Head Tim McIntyre was alerted to the videos by a blogger who had seen them. Bloggers at Consumerist.com used clues in the video to find the franchise location. They spread that news and forced the franchise to bring in the local health department. And local health advised that all the stock of food be thrown away.

As the company learned about the video, Domino's executives initially decided not to respond very much in the social media, hoping the controversy would quiet down. That misreading of the situation is illustrated by their later comments: "What we missed was the perpetual mushroom effect of viral sensations"; "if you think it's not going to spread, that's when it gets bigger"; "we were doing and saying things, but they weren't being covered in Twitter."

After a few days, Domino's did create its own Twitter account to address the comments, and it presented its chief executive on YouTube. "It elevated to a point where just responding isn't good enough." The company had to proactively develop a full blown response both off *and* online using PR for the press and writing up almost every hour how things were progressing. The controversy came as a shock to Domino's, but they now monitor all relevant channels, all the time. But they also take the initiative with all this, letting the world know about the good things that are happening too.

As Warren Buffet has said: "it takes 20 years to build a reputation and five minutes to ruin it. If you think about that, you'll do things differently."

And so the message is that brand marketers need now to think and plan for their Brand for this multi-channel world. Even if some initial analysis suggests that the Brand is indeed not one that is typically gossiped and commented on, one bad PR mix-up, in any channel and, as the folk at Domino's saw, reputations can come crashing very quickly.

6   How Ready is your Organization to Become an Effective MCE?

How developed is your organization as a multi-channel enterprise (MCE)? Becoming an effective MCE may well require a major transformational and strategic change. It is not just about opening a Twitter account and putting the CEO on YouTube. It's not just about active brand reputation and sentiment monitoring. It won't be enough to set up a Facebook page. All those tactical activities will count for nothing unless there is a clear long-term and strategic plan about how the company should be taking advantage of not just the multi-channel environment but digital technology generally. And that will mean examining opportunities to use web technology tools: whether to take advantage, for example, of the Cloud, whether to automate and outsource certain tasks, what skills and expertise will be required for the future, what technology platforms and architectures will best enable the company to compete as a winner as this decade unfolds. No matter what the industry sector, no matter what the customer base, web technology is going to be a major driving force for change. No company will be able to ignore this and any that do will fail. There is absolutely no question about that.

And the key is to understand that this will take time – it is a journey along a path similar to that shown in Figure 3.

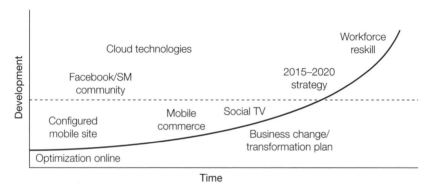

Figure 3   **Development of an MCE**

It is impossible to short-circuit this journey or skip steps or rush through things to try to catch up. That just won't work. It's going to be a total process involving the whole company. By definition, an effective and winning MCE cannot be achieved by one department or one team. It will require the commitment, prioritization and leadership of the CEO and the executive committee. It will require tough decision-making as budgets and resources get reallocated to provide a balanced MCE approach. Most especially, the ability for everyone in the company to have a single but cross-channel view of the customer will require new technology tools and platforms and the migration away from mainframe to desktop, from client server to Cloud, from functional architecture to SOA (service-oriented architecture), from C++ to open source web-based solutions, from years of development to months of agility, from a few big multi-million dollar corporate projects to numerous but coordinated IT initiatives. It will require a "tech-watch" capability that invests in understanding the latest tools and technology opportunities, not necessarily to be at leading edge all the time, but to be able to operate in the vanguard rather than bringing up the rear. It will require a commitment to transform the company from the old to the new – from "traditional" approaches to becoming MCE-led – and it will involve a clear vision to establish a compelling strategy to win in 2015 and beyond.

So, how far along this journey is your organization? The box opposite presents a template for change. For each question, create a score out of 10. The score should reflect the degree to which the organization is responding to or already tackling the respective challenge or opportunity.

The total available score is 200. A score of anything less than 100 should cause significant concern. It would suggest the company is just shutting its eyes to the changing world. At the other extreme, a score of 150-plus may show we've discovered a winner. In this book, we will continue to review case examples of companies who are achieving a degree of excellence in their MCE journey. What distinguishes them is their own awareness and recognition that transformation takes time and that there are many steps in the journey towards any final completion. (Example: Kodak started their transformation in 2003/04 and, 8 years later, stated publicly that it will take at least a further 3 or 4 years of continued hard commitment and effort.)

But what is important in using a questionnaire of this sort is that it poses the key and most difficult questions. It can be set up to draw a line in the sand, to establish a benchmark. It can be targeted separately at each function, at each business unit, in each geographical area. It can be used as an annual trends and progress check. It can measure the degree to which a company is transforming … and where it stands on that journey.

Becoming an MCE – A Template for Change

Score

A. Strategic

1 Is the expression "Multi-Channel Enterprise" or "MCE" used at all across the company? ☐

2 Is it used in lots of different functions and departments? (e.g. it's still common today for MCE to be the language of the Marketing department only) ☐

3 Is there any definition or scoping as to what MCE means for your specific company? ☐

4 Is there any sense of timeframe or a roadmap for how an MCE effective organization might be established? ☐

5 Is this anywhere near the CEO's priority agenda? ☐

B. Costs and Benefits

6 Making the change to an MCE will be time-consuming and incur significant transformation costs, especially in IT and skills-training. Has any analysis been done for your company as to what these transformational costs might be? ☐

7 Considerable investment will be required, has that total been quantified over time? ☐

8 The return on this investment, however, could be very high. Has that been quantified at all? ☐

C. Competitors

9 Have any rival companies made any moves in this MCE direction such that it's acting as a further catalyst for your organization to change? ☐

D. Market place customers

10 To what extent is there interest or pressure from customers to become a more effective MCE? ☐

E. Technology

11 Does the company have visionary leadership in its Technology team? ☐

12 Is their voice heard or is it stuck in a back-office project room? ☐

13 Would the company describe itself as being technology-led? ☐

14 Are there sufficient resources and investments available for technology improvements? ☐

15 Is there any capability and insight that captures for senior management the changes that are taking place in technology solutions? ☐

F. Data

16 Is there any collection of data that monitors or reports on customers' multi-channel transactions and activities? ☐

17 Is any insight being derived from the data as to trends and evolving behavior? ☐

18 Is there any initiative to collect and distil this data in real time? ☐

G. Multi-channel cooperation

19 Is there a permanent grouping or committee or team or department in the company that has an MCE remit today? ☐

20 Are there any examples, either within your own company or competitors', which show where an MCE approach has paid back? ☐

7 Mobile Comms, Content and Commerce

After much hype and expectation, the mobile/cell phone has finally "taken off". At last this device has started to live up to expectations. Apple, with its touch screen magic, has proved to have the initiative to capture everyone's attention and imagination (Plate 4). And other smart phone providers have rushed to copy.

The stats are extraordinary:

▷ The Apple iPhone is the fastest new tech selling device in history! And it has an unrivalled application eco-system with global support and reach. It sold 6.1 million original units over five quarters from launch in the US in summer 2007 to roll-out through 2008 into 22 countries. Sales in the fourth quarter of 2008 surpassed temporarily those of RIM's Blackberry, which briefly made Apple the third largest mobile phone manufacturer by revenue, after Nokia and Samsung. Approximately 6.4 million iPhones are active in the US alone. Sales growth continues – by the start of fiscal year 2011 a total of 73.5 million iPhones had been sold. The company expected to ship 20 million iPhones in just the first quarter of 2011. According to Strategy Analytics, if the iPhone continues at this rate of sale it is set to establish itself as the second largest selling smart phone in the world, ahead of the Blackberry and Samsung versions and just behind Nokia which, despite its problems, still manages to leverage its powerful global distribution to maintain overall market leadership (BBC News).
▷ The number of UK users of all smart phones grew 58% in the 12 months following the launch of the iPhone (Comscore).
▷ UK consumers proved once again that they are among the most eager adopters of new technologies by using their newly acquired smart

phone as a prime social networking tool. Users accessing Facebook or blogs via their mobile grew 71% through 2010 and into 2011 (Comscore Mobilens).

▷ In both the UK and the US consumers are "lapping up mobile content"; nearly half say that they regularly use their mobile/cell phone in this way (NMA).

▷ Similar growth has been seen elsewhere in Europe with an increase of 41% in smart phone adoption (Comscore).

▷ 650 million people worldwide now access the mobile internet. In some countries mobile is the main access route, e.g. in India about 60% of internet users go through mobile devices (MobiThinking).

▷ Mobile retailing has started to explode (according to 2011 reports produced separately by the BBC and Google) with almost one-third of shoppers in the UK saying they have used an m-commerce site to find out product info, compare prices and complete transactions (*Marketing*).

▷ Since Gap introduced the Stream iPad app, it has found that 45% of users who view a product this way proceed to the checkout.

The smart phone has reached critical mass. And we are just a step away from a whole series of further innovations and applications which will continue to energize and encourage the use of the mobile phone as the principal device for communications, content and multi-channel commerce.

We can get an immediate understanding of what this future mobile world will look like by exploring what already goes on in Japan today.

▷ Japan has 108 million mobile phone subscribers, which is 95% of the youth/adult population.

▷ 9 out of 10 are mobile web access users.

▷ 90% access at least once a day.

▷ 61% of users aged 15 to 50 access hourly!

▷ Almost everyone is on 3G fast networks, typically messaging is free and contracts are based on flat-rate data plans.

▷ Some $20bn of mobile commerce is forecast for 2011 and that splits about 40% purchase of goods, 30% purchase of services and the balance on various other items, e.g. auctions, gambling etc.

▷ The key reasons why the mobile is popular for m-commerce are: (i) "it's quick to download" and (ii) "mobile purchasing is made easy."

▷ Customers can pay by attaching the cost to their mobile phone bill, by credit card or at local store pay points.

▷ The most popular categories for purchasing are (in order): fashion clothing, books, DVDs, music, cosmetics, food and travel.

▷ Factors driving growth include:

– use of the phone camera to capture a digital image of the product and then immediately search on the mobile for m-commerce stores selling that item at the cheapest price.

- the popularity of Mobile TV and the now well-established built-in in-program product shopping.
- barcode and coupon promotion scanning or downloads and usage, e.g. buy a McDonald's meal.
- NFC (near field communications) technology has been widely adopted and built into most handsets to provide short range wireless connectivity. Touch or place your mobile near a terminal and pay or use it as an ID card or as a general comms tool.

Source: Barclaycard

Japan presently leads the world in mobile connectivity, web surfing and application use. While the US leads in terms of accessing social networks and blogs and Europeans love text messaging, Japanese users will snap photos, watch TV or video and are already accustomed to using the phone as a preferred micro payment device. In fact, so widespread and embedded is the use of the mobile in Japan that latest marketing efforts are now targeting the 5- to 9-year-old age group. Usage among that segment is expected to reach 64% in 2011. And while in Japan the hot social network is Mixi instead of Facebook and people prefer Gree to YouTube, everyone loves Twitter!

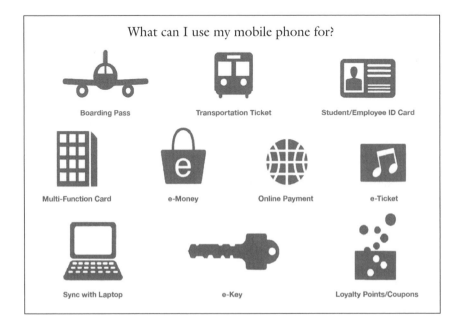

What can I use my mobile phone for?

Boarding Pass	Transportation Ticket	Student/Employee ID Card
Multi-Function Card	e-Money	Online Payment	e-Ticket
Sync with Laptop	e-Key	Loyalty Points/Coupons

Telcos, ISPs, network operators, handset manufacturers, Brand owners and distributors in other Asian tigers like South Korea, Thailand, China and India are all looking enviously at the developed Japanese m-commerce infrastructure and success, and examining ways that they can also move to capture some of the same commercial opportunity.

In South Korea, government protection of local handset manufacturers LG and Samsung has prevented the introduction of foreign smart phones, and the Apple iPhone only launched with limited distribution support at the start of 2010. But we can expect a lot of catch-up activity and investment in that country. Korea used to lead the world in mobile phone technology and is keen not to fall too far behind. It has been committed to rolling out its own domestic mobile solution called WiBro (wireless broadband) but problems with that 4G network technology have been slow to get resolved. The new smart phones will use an adaptation and upgrade of more proven and reliable existing 3G technology and are expected to gain wider acceptance more quickly.

In China there are in 2011 already some 400 million mobile phone users but this is mostly for voice and simple data transfer. The number of subscribers is forecast to reach 1 billion by 2020. That would likely include some 80% of the youth/adult population. Unlike Korea which has grown up with a very strong PC internet culture, China does not have that fixed infrastructure and so mobile usage and take-up is expected to be quicker and reach higher levels of penetration. The limitation will be how much of the country will be covered by the likely 4G technology that is adopted and rolls out. At present only about 55% of the population is covered. That will be the key driver of the numbers that can achieve internet access. That and the government's interest in regulating content will ultimately determine the size of the m-commerce market.

Looking more broadly, ABI Research forecast that by 2015, across the world, some $120bn worth of goods and services will be purchased via a mobile phone. And ABI go on to point out that, even appreciating that most internet-related forecasts are somewhat ambitious and ahead of actual take-up, nevertheless they have mostly proved right over the long term. The parallels here with early Web 1.0 forecasts cannot be ignored. Research Houses like Gartner, Jupiter and Forrester all made what appeared at the time to be forecasts full of hype and hubris. But they have of course ultimately proved conservative in their predictions over the long term!

This kind of growth and development is all dependent on continuing mobile technology advances and it's important just to stand back for a moment and review what's going on across the world.

4G is currently the major innovation. 4G (4th generation) is the name given to the radio network frequency that's used by the phone. It is already used and available in Japan and in the US. For example Sprint in the US claims its network can provide about one-third of the population with a 4G signal. And in May 2010, Germany completed its local auction of licenses to use the 4G radio spectrum.

4G is attractive because it provides super fast speeds of around 3 to 6 megabits per second. And that is around 10 times the speed of the average 3G connection which it is replacing. 4G does provide a very slick and quick user experience and naturally encourages further widespread usage and adoption and more interest in all the available tools and functions. "4G takes us up to 100 mbps and then potentially on to a gigabit per second," comments the Head of Mobile at Accenture, Stuart Orr.

However, moving to 4G will not be without its delays and roadblocks. Apart from the need for governments to formally allocate the spectrum and licenses, there is then the investment cost to be borne by the network operators themselves and critically, too, the time it takes to establish or adapt the mast signal network. Once such an infrastructure is in place then handset manufacturers are usually quick to introduce the new handsets that can exploit it. But this can all take a number of years to fully roll out. For example, although 4G has been available since 2010 in the US, Apple has taken its time to move from the proven 3G network. Its Apple iPhone 5 was scheduled to launch on 4G in the US only in the summer of 2011.

Meantime, the UK and most of Europe are working within their established 3G environment. And while 3G is certainly much faster than what it replaced (imaginatively known as 2G!), it is not fast enough for the latest applications such as music streaming, watching movies or making video calls. In addition the 3G networks are running out of room! Research by investment house BNP Paribas predicts that by 2013 networks in city centers across Europe just won't be able to cope! Figure 4 shows how video is driving the rapid growth in mobile internet traffic which is predicted to rise 39-fold between 2009 and 2014.

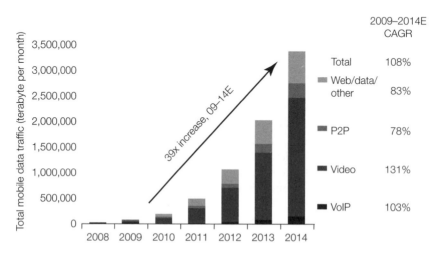

Data source: Cisco Visual Networking Index: Global Mobile Data Traffic Forecast Update, 2009–2014

Figure 4   **Global mobile data traffic by type, 2008–2014**
Source: Morgan Stanley.

It's either a case of moving to 4G or adopting a hybrid called LTE (Long Term Evolution), which is essentially an upgrade to the existing 3G network. It does not provide the same speeds as 4G but it is quicker than the current solution, can provide further network capacity and, perhaps most importantly, will be quicker and relatively cheaper to implement than 4G. (This is an important consideration, of course, with budgets and costs under considerable pressure in the first part of this decade.) Nevertheless, telco consultancy Aircom estimated it would take close to $750m and a 12-month implementation program for a UK operator to upgrade to an LTE network, so it is still a substantial commitment in time and resource. But this estimate quickly came to be regarded by some commentators as on the high side when equipment costs came down because of supplier competition from Ericsson, Alcatel and Motorola among others. Meantime in recognition of growing demand and pressure on connectivity, the UK has joined the group of countries looking to establish a 4G environment. They will auction new licenses for that spectrum in 2012.

LTE is itself already up and running in the European theater with some six different networks. For example, in Sweden, TeliaSonera is offering LTE mobile handsets providing, it claims, up to 10mbs. Vodafone launched LTE in Germany in 2011, and is using that as its European test bed before deciding to roll out elsewhere. And France Telecom has LTE trials across several regions in France through 2011 (even while expecting bids for its own 4G licenses).

While network operators are fighting for share of the next generation mobile, meantime the device and hardware war continues unabated. This has reached a new level of intensity following the sudden and rapid rise of the smart phone. So 2011 saw a number of new product launches:

▷ Google is pushing its Android operating system that works on devices from Samsung, Motorola and others. It has claimed that it is now the No. 3 mobile operating system, ahead of Apple and just behind Nokia and Blackberry (using Comscore data for Q4 2010).

▷ Samsung announced a new series of tablets and smart phones for launch in 2011/12.

▷ In response Microsoft, whose operating system market share continues to struggle and is well behind Google and Apple, has launched Windows 7 OS for Mobile. Of course Microsoft are so keen to push other parts of their organization onto the home screen, from Bing to Zune to X-Box, that their semi-walled approach does tend to influence the type of user that chooses their products.

▷ Microsoft's announcement of a "global strategic partnership" with Nokia can be expected to both accelerate the adoption of the Microsoft OS but to generate a new wave of smart phone initiatives from the combined group.

▷ The iPhone 5 4G phone will launch during the course of 2011. At the time of writing, the phone was expected to offer features that can take advantage of the faster speeds, so expect video chat as a possible new killer app, face recognition security and streaming movies and TV functions. The phone design is slimmer at just 9.3mm thin and will have further extended battery life of up to 14 hours.

▷ Blackberry has launched their answer to the iPad, the Playbook. It was available in the USA from Q1 2011 and then rolled out to other countries during the course of 2011. It uses 4G in the US so it is ahead of the tablet game in that respect, and its slightly smaller size means that, unlike the iPad, it can fit into your pocket. It also features a port for a hands-free or Bluetooth device so you can make calls. Perhaps the Playbook is still too big to replace the phone but certainly it enables people on the move to essentially operate through one piece of kit if they want to.

▷ AT&T, T-Mobile and Verizon have announced the formation of a joint venture to build ISIS, a national m-commerce network for the US. The aim is to provide a mobile payment function that enables all mobile phones to make point of sale purchases. They will partner with Barclaycard in the US to provide a secure credit card "mobile wallet". It will use NFC technology; touching or placing your phone near a terminal will automatically trigger the payment. Additional security such as PIN number entry is also being looked at. It's planned that ISIS will eliminate the need to carry your credit card with you. It can also carry reward cards, coupons, travel and other tickets and passes.

▷ Orange and Barclaycard have announced plans to trial a system in the UK and France that will utilize the NFC approach to allow customers to make payments by touching their phone to compatible electronic readers. The challenge here will be that existing SIM cards don't typically have the NFC technology, so that evolution needs to unfold as handsets are upgraded. However retailers are racing to trial this new, quicker, easier way of paying for things. It's likely to be especially targeted at "micropayments" where the value is less than $20. Retailers in the UK, including McDonald's, Eat, Boots, Yo! Sushi, Tesco and Live Concert festival "Live Nation", will all be exploring how NFC can be used to boost sales. What's more, with the mobile's GPS location-tracking facility consumers can be additionally targeted with local coupons and promotions to further encourage this extended greater mobile phone usage.

All this supplier activity and investment will naturally and inevitably lead to substantial further growth worldwide in mobile connectivity and extended usage. It feeds the consumers' appetite for the convenience of anytime anyhow on-the-move internet and communications access. And the increased functionality and reliability gives further comfort and confidence.

As the Morgan Stanley analysis in Figure 5 shows, average iPhone usage per day in the US is 50% higher than its predecessor, increasing from 40 to 60 minutes, and most critically that extra time is being invested not just in voice but also in the whole range of other mobile applications from games

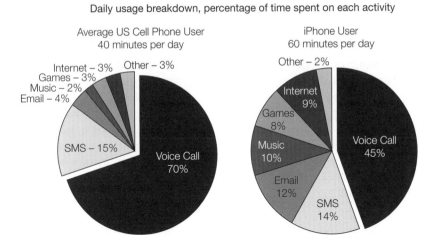

Daily usage breakdown, percentage of time spent on each activity

Note: CTIA estimates average voice call time per day is 27 minutes, assuming 70% of total time spent is on voice call, per iSuppli, total average time spent on cell phone is approx. 40 minutes per day. iPhone time spent per day is our estimates.

Data source: iSuppli Consumer Trak survey, 10/08, Morgan Stanley Research.

Figure 5   **iPhone usage**

Source: Morgan Stanley

and gambling, email, music and general internet access. In fact, mobile phone usage is increasingly about data not voice: for a cell phone the average was 70% voice while for an iPhone it is only 45%.

As a result Brands are starting to look ever more closely at where their internet traffic is coming from and e-commerce operators are realizing that the phone has become a vital component in their multi-channel communications and engagement with their customers.

For many Brands, the first stage of this engagement has been to develop an App. That may be a somewhat crude and simplistic response, but it can be done quickly and it can also capture some good PR and headlines. Such a move is not a long-term substitute for a carefully planned mobile internet strategy and a properly configured-for-mobile web presence and site, but it has got a number of brands up and running and into the mobile world. In particular, early leaders have proven the power of the device to generate further sales growth:

▷ Taobao.com has established itself as an early global leader in mobile commerce. It's the equivalent of eBay in China and racked up close to $1bn in revenues in 2010/11.

▷ Close behind Taobao is Amazon. Jeff Bezos has announced that his company had achieved $800m of sales from customers accessing Amazon from their mobile phone.

▷ eBay has announced that it is experiencing high levels of mobile phone trading and forecasts growth to some $1.5bn in gross merchandise volume in 2011. This is up 140% on the previous year. In fact eBay has found that it is selling one car every five minutes via mobile services and is processing one transaction on a mobile each second!

▷ Mobile retail in the context of m-coupon redemption values in the US is expected to reach $15bn in 2015 according to Jupiter.

▷ A recent survey by the IAB and IMRG (Interactive Media Retail Group) found that 41% of UK retailers expect to have a transactional mobile site in place in 2011. The main finding was a complete shift in emphasis from perceiving the mobile as not much more than a shop front/brochureware at best to leading retailers treating it as a core part of their multi-channel sales strategy.

On the supply side, the UK has fallen a bit behind the US in the development of m-commerce. There is no equivalent of the ISIS-type initiative (except for the limited Orange/Barclaycard trial) in which network operators are combining to create the secure mobile wallet. But consumer demand and expectation, together with the strong view that NFC technology will be a huge source and driver of growth, will mean that many more developments can be anticipated.

That said, there is still some way to go till businesses universally embrace this mobile potential. Econsultancy research found that more than 50% of business managers had not checked the appearance of their website on mobile browsers. Of those who had checked, 41% admitted that their site "did not look good"! and only 21% said they had budgeted plans to do anything about this during the coming 12 months! The research highlighted the need for more urgency in terms of configuring websites for mobile and, more generally, developing a clear mobile strategy and presence. Given the expected level of consumer demand, the return on investment in this area should be there.

And indeed, demand-side activity driven, for example, by shopping-hungry, internet-loving UK consumers is ramping up fast. The IAB conducted a survey of 1000 people across the UK at the end of 2010. They found that 43% surfed the internet from their mobile on a regular basis specifically to look up product information and compare prices; 40% looked for location-specific information about opening times and address details for a particular high street store; 37% went on to say that they had used their phone to make payments principally by adding something directly to their mobile phone bill or by credit card. The survey also found that people were much more likely to buy a product if they could quickly and easily find out information about it on their mobile phone. The conclusion was a wake-up call to suppliers, brands and retailers: your target market and consumer wants the facility of m-commerce, so gear up to provide it!

Let's see what's available so far:

(i) Tesco launched a transactional mobile site just before Christmas 2010. They made headlines because it was configured for use only on a Nokia phone in the starter phase. That decision was based on research that showed their target customer, the B C1 C2 shopper, typically did not have an iPhone and was more likely to have something less expensive to buy and run. The product range is drawn from Tesco Direct which is their non-food operation selling consumer electronics. Tesco mobile is seen as a key stage in the development of their multi-channel strategy. They have found that people will research high value items and will want to share and discuss them with friends and family. They have set up the mobile site to facilitate this and to enable subsequent purchase, and expect to introduce functions like order and reserve for later purchase and/or collection in-store. Already, 500,000 visitors a month are accessing the site via mobile browsers and that number is predicted to grow.

The key innovator at Tesco has been Nick Lansley who is their Head of R&D. He blogs regularly, acknowledges customer feedback and openly shares plans and next-stage developments. 2011 has seen the launch of a Groceries/Food app, again on Nokia only to start with, but enabling Tesco to test the ground with this and also experiment with the commercial attractiveness of Nokia's Ovi Store. While such "walled gardens" have plummeted in usage and popularity, they still play a prominent role in network operators' enhanced revenue plans and can be influential in directing traffic from the mobile screen home page. The Food app has now been repurposed and made available on the iPhone and phones using Windows 7. Tesco recognizes the need to be customer-driven and caters for people who are overwhelmingly time-poor and busy, those with a very strong desire for things that make their life more convenient.

(ii) Marks & Spencer has made some early and clear decisions about what it wants to achieve through the mobile. It has not launched any apps but, instead, it has reconfigured a version of its website to make it effective on the major browsers. Sienne Veit, who heads up Business Development, comments that their plans were based on a great deal of analysis and the finding that nearly 1 million people had visited the regular website from their mobile. The number of different types of phones runs into the hundreds, so Marks & Spencer decided to develop their mobile site rather than create different apps for different phones. They use the same payment system on the mobile as on the e-commerce site because customers prefer to use the same unified account. People shop for much the same sort of things on both sites and the mobile average order value is not that different from the full web order value.

(iii)   Waitrose, part of the John Lewis department store chain, has launched both an app and a mobile website. The app gives access to a wide variety of content from celebrity chefs' recipes to product promotions. There's also a store locator which uses GPS to quickly identify the nearest shop. Perhaps too keen to add functions and variety, the app also has a food timer, a weight conversion chart (kilos to pounds), a vintage wine guide, a matching list of wine and food, nutritional information, a shopping list plus a selection of how-to videos (and the kitchen sink!).

(iv)   Other retailers with similar initiatives, either just launched or in the works, include DIY retailer B&Q, Boots, Net-a-Porter (whose app has won awards for its easy use and constantly changing but deliberately limited selection of clothing to buy), Next clothing and electricals retailer Comet. Comet's mobile website allows for product browsing and reserving items for in-store viewing and collection, but as yet it has no purchasing facility.

Retailers, especially, are facing the choice of whether to develop an app or a website for mobile, or both. Some like M&S have opted for the website-only approach. Others like Waitrose have tried to cover all the bases and thrown initial investment and resource down both routes. Most will see the app as something that can deliver initial appeal and provide a nice and easy way to access content. But most will soon realize that, whether they maintain and update their apps or not, the longer term must embrace the fully configured website. Apps need to be developed for each mobile OS, and what works on Apple does not work on Android. In addition, while development for Apple will work on all iPhones, development for Android will need some additional tailoring, depending on the handset manufacturer. And in the same way, what works on Samsung will not necessarily work as well on all HTC phones. Therefore, the development time and expense for widespread reach, rather than just simply garnering a brief headline in the trade press, can be considerable.

Developing an m-commerce website will simply give a wider and more immediate reach. It's more easily optimized and so found through a search engine. It does not need to be downloaded or separately found and paid for. It does not require third party approval. (For example, in early 2011 there was a waiting time of up to 6 weeks for an iPhone app to be considered and approved, and there may be a requirement for further development work to resolve any glitches or to meet Apple's latest guidelines before it can go live.) It also avoids the high commission/revenue share costs payable, e.g. to Apple for user access through its devices and OS.

Long term, most commentators agree that the browser-based mobile web market will grow faster and so getting the mobile site right is going to be the key. Mobile Marketing Association chief Paul Berney believes that retailers need to consider how best to integrate mobile at potentially a number of different stages in the customer purchase decision-making journey. A good mobile offering will not only help to drive footfall, it will also help to engage with shoppers and it can be a key way of staying in touch after the purchase has been made.

What are these stages that Paul Berney is referring to? Reflecting a likely sales engagement cycle we might expect to see the following mobile interaction opportunities:

Product search
▼
Price comparison
▼
Peer review
▼
Coupon/promotion incentive
▼
Store locator
▼
Brand contact/call center
▼
Purchase
▼
Sales satisfaction check
▼
Loyalty program

Research shows that the purchase process typically starts with a product search. If the brand is well-known some will skip the generic search and go straight to the mobile site, and that can be encouraged of course by general brand-building and customer awareness. Price checks and peer reviews have become increasingly important influences for e- and m-shopping so it's very useful to facilitate that. Finding ways to bookmark key product info pages, sending links to friends, accessing existing product and brand reviews and comparisons will all help to facilitate the selection process. Bearing in mind the multi-channel world in which all this activity takes place, it's again going to be important to have functions like store finder and contact. And how about a "reserve this for me at my nearest store for 24 hours" option? Finally, purchasing and the check-out process need to work slickly with the fewest possible steps. And that's why M&S are using a unified check-out system so that if you are already registered on the website that registration could be carried over to the phone. And it's why the ISIS initiative from AT&T and Verizon could prove powerful – it may enable mobile phone users to purchase using a pre-set pre-registered wallet. Why not provide some version of Amazon's market-leading "one-click" order process? And finally how easy is it to stay in touch with customers by sending them text alerts, coupons, promotion messages? Provided this is synced up and complementary to any e-commerce/email type loyalty-building activity then it can offer a lot of opportunity for customer relationship development. You have their email, their mobile number and probably their postal address. That richness of data should enable plenty of productive interaction!

The effectiveness of many of these interactions can also be enhanced by taking advantage of location-based mobile services. Most phones sold in recent years come with GPS (Global Positioning System). GPS uses a simple communications chip that links with satellites in space and can provide pinpoint data about the location of you and your mobile. While critics claim this is an invasion of individual privacy with Big Brother "watching over you", nevertheless GPS is rapidly becoming a popular piece of mobile phone functionality. Users either opt-in automatically when they set up their phone (GPS typically has to be actively switched off rather than on) or are encouraged to do so by a growing array of mobile marketing promotions and apps that use GPS software.

"Location-based marketing", or "LBM" as it's becoming known, is a marketer's dream. A brand can now in effect target the right consumers not only with the right message but also when they are in the right place at the right time! So now product searches and store locator checks for example can all be made much more immediately relevant. If a brand has a GPS app or function link on its mobile website then a consumer can straight away find location-relevant and specific information. Combine that with social networking tools and you can find friends, show where you are, choose the best nearest bar, get directions, arrange to meet, access local information like the nearest bus station and times of buses, and all the searches and messaging can be focused on finding what's most relevant to where you are. You don't need to know the name of the street, town or map coordinates! Your phone does it all for you.

Marketers will need to find the balance in deploying "push" driven GPS messaging: "Now we know you're near our store here's a coupon you can use." That can be very effective but it can also be regarded as intrusive and annoying, and blogs and forums can quickly circulate critical comment about a brand's perhaps too-aggressive marketing activities. The alternative is the more subtle "pull" approach. This might include a location-based banner ad in a smart phone application that can encourage you to find out local store/entertainment-type information. It could also include something like the "Check-in" feature on Foursquare.

Foursquare is marketed as a location-based social networking world. It's most popular use is as a mobile phone app. You scan in, for example, your smart phone address book of friends and followers on Facebook or Twitter. When you "check-in" Foursquare will tell all your friends who are nearby (typically within around a 250-yard radius). Foursquare goes on to then give you information about local events and places to go to, for example, cafes, bars and restaurants. (And that's where they make their money, providing that information listing with some banners at the top or bottom and some highlighted and flashing as "new".)

While initiatives like Foursquare might sound intrusive they are in fact extremely popular. (There's a similar venture called ShopKick which is much more explicit brand and store promotion location service.) The IAB has conducted a recent survey that shows that 70% of users are happy to readily share location details. They feel that the value information they get back, whether it's the nearest bar or where their nearest friends are, makes that "intrusion" worthwhile. And they are even readier to share if they are in an application, for example, looking at content on the Gap mobile site or their app, and this additional location-based info can be made available.

Providers are rushing to provide "location-based services" to exploit this niche. Google has launched Hyperlocal. As their own promotion material says: "Think of it as smart advertising. It knows where you are, and everything around you via your Android phone's GPS. You search for something you want or need, and Google can now serve you a relevant ad based on both your search and GPS coordinates." O2, the mobile phone operator, offers its own service which is available on all types of handsets. They provide a location triangulation service which identifies the position of the phone in relation to three nearby cell towers. O2 offers a specific opt-in service which will send you promotional ads and info relating to the areas of registered interest. Verizon is investing in this space with a $10m injection into start-up Geodelic which is establishing a location-based mobile platform for brands. It also provides GeoGuides that give additional layers of information about searched-for locations, for example, local info on what is around an airport, best hotels by category etc. Rippll is a specialist location-based marketing company which, for example, has worked with TGI Friday and seen substantial interest and "click through" during a targeted ad campaign. Meantime, Facebook has launched its "Places" service which allows the site's users to opt-in and disclose their current location. In return they can both better communicate with friends who are nearby and also they can receive messages from stores and brands with local buying ideas.

Coffee shops are perhaps a natural for this type of prospective customer targeting and location-specific communication and incentive. With most streets and malls full of coffee shops and diners, they are all chasing the same customer whose choice of coffee is often impulsive and spur-of-the-moment.

Starbucks have been an early pioneer of location-based marketing in an effort to win that impulsive customer choice. It has trialed apps on the iPhone. MyStarbucks enables you to use the phone's GPS to find the nearest store. And it also allows you to refill a Starbucks card, get discounts, get free refills and two hours of free Wi-Fi. It is also testing a mobile application which will use a barcode to replace the plastic card.

"We're really venturing into new waters in terms of mobile payment," says Starbucks' Stephen Gillett. Mobile payment using the phone and a downloaded or scanned-in barcode is commonplace in countries like Japan and South Korea. So

Source: Starbucks

far this has not really caught on elsewhere but it is all very simple to do. At Starbucks one in seven transactions already involves either a gift or loyalty card and Stephen Gillett considers that "a significant amount of our traffic [is] represented by loyalty cards of some sort".

All this mobile opportunity does not stand alone. A mobile marketing campaign without anything else will have some, but probably quite a limited, effect. The key is to see all this in the context of a full multi-channel and integrated communications plan. With c.15% of all retail sales expected to be influenced by mobile applications (Booz & Company), this will mean some $300bn of revenues are at stake across the US, UK, France and Germany. And by 2015, Booz forecasts that as many as half of all consumers will use their smart phones as part of their shopping process. According to Kevin Ertell and Larry Freed of ForeSee Results: "Any retailer [that is] not actively working to develop, measure and refine its customers' mobile experience is leaving money on the table for competitors … It's true that mobile sites have far less maturity than traditional e-retail websites … [but that probably does not matter] to consumers. Their expectations are being set by the best websites and the best mobile experiences. They aren't going to have a lot of patience for excuses about the challenges that mobile shopping presents when it come to design and usability." Good experiences on mobile sites encourage shoppers to return to that retailer. To quote Kevin Ertell again, "It's a reminder … that every customer touch point matters to overall loyalty and sales. Retailers cannot afford to ignore or neglect the mobile experience and assume it won't hurt their traditional online or in-store business."

AutoTrader provides an example of one organization that is leading the field in this mobile and multi-channel approach to customer engagement. Launched in 1996, the website is now the leading site for buying and selling cars online, carrying thousands of car ads. While there is a similar business in the US, the award-winning UK operation each month receives around 11 million unique visitors who carry out more than 100 million searches on new and used cars. AutoTrader set up their first mobile site as early as 2006, implemented a dot mobi version in 2008 and in 2009 reconfigured to establish a mobile site which could work on numerous different handsets and browsers. In 2010 they launched specific smart phone apps making it easier to search for cars, for example, on an iPhone. They have also started up their own social media networking. Aside from setting up the standard Facebook page and encouraging chat on Twitter, they have instigated specific campaigns to broaden their audience reach and interaction. Their promotion "hid" five golden keys each day and if you found one you had a chance to win £1000. The keys were hidden variously on the website, inside the magazine, on the mobile website and in the iPhone app. Clues were placed on Facebook and on Twitter, encouraging you to hunt down the keys. Clues could also be found, for example, in the magazine which directed you to search the mobile website, say. So the whole approach was to drive awareness and reach across the whole multi-channel environment.

The results showed that there were more than 1.5 million searches for clues and c. 40% of them took place via the mobile, whether searching the e-commerce or the mobile website. Mobile traffic was 40% up on the previous month. According to Matt Thompson and others at AutoTrader, the promotion enhanced perceptions of AutoTrader as a dynamic brand that you can interact with on the move. AutoTrader did not just jump into mobile and multi-channel marketing. They spent several years learning and developing, and have begun to understand through ongoing research what their consumers want and what will work. Past mistakes have been important in helping the learning process and in fine-tuning their approach. Mobile is in its infancy and AutoTrader see these initiatives as just a starting point.

8 "It All Pivots Around Social Media"

The Centre for Retail Research (CRR) predicts that e-commerce will bring European retailers some €2bn each month on average through 2011. That's a 23% increase versus the previous year. Meantime, spending in shops in expected to stay flat with at best a 0.5% increase forecast. With e-commerce now the norm and in fact the only growth option, what will be the next evolution and how should retailers capitalize upon and maintain that e-commerce momentum? The answer, according to the CRR: "It all pivots around social media".

Social media (SM) has become a phenomenon that ranks alongside the advent of the smart phone. It is revolutionizing communications. It is changing the way companies do business. It is materially influencing day-to-day communications. It is impacting governments and countries. It is reaching millions and there are no boundaries. It is not just that people of all ages and demographics are engaged. It involves people across the world, from the most sophisticated countries to developing nations, from the US to Iraq, from the UK to China, from fixed line to mobile, from Facebook and MySpace in the West to Orkut in Brazil and QZone in China.

That this has happened should be no surprise. It's one of the "killer apps" the internet was invented for. To enable the sharing of ideas and information, to collaborate, to establish or widen communities, to reach out beyond the traditional boundaries of a school, institution, city or country and to build networks of contacts from all sources anywhere and everywhere. What has been surprising is the sheer speed of this development, the degree to which it has been taken up and the now unstoppable momentum that it has built. This is without doubt a key part of our future world. It may evolve into different formats and more specialist communities, it may engage with new technology tools and in more visual ways but it is here to stay.

In the rush to jump onto the SM bandwagon, it's been quickly forgotten how recent is this innovation online. Despite the parade of so-called experts proclaiming to know all about SM and how to be a success in it and what its next evolution will be, the phenomenon is still in its infancy, having just learnt to walk. Heaven knows what will happen when it hits its teenage years!

It was only in the first half of 2009 that MySpace and then Facebook really began to grab attention and started seeing real community traction. The number of Facebook users in January 2008 was around 100 million, in January 2009 that number had risen to 150 million. But it was only through 2009 that we started seeing the amazing penetration of the Facebook world, with the number of users growing to 360 million by the end of that year. In 2011 at 600 million users, we have entered a realm of size and reach which is hard to imagine. And what is even more amazing is that half of the 600 million typically visit the site every day. That is every day! And the average amount of time spent is around an hour each day. This is so unique, so different to any other site that the stats have no comparison. Others may boast of millions of unique visitors but their numbers are much much smaller. Amazon and eBay top the polls of the most visited commercial website with around 80 million global visitors and 70 million, respectively, per month. However, those visitors will typically visit on average two or three times per month and spend on average a total of 30 minutes on the site during the whole month. Find some of the biggest UK retail sites and we're looking at on average 10 million per month on Tesco and Argos, again two or three visits per month with average time spent of about 30 minutes in total per month. Facebook just dwarfs this. And so it's no wonder it's become a major attraction to brands and marketers and retailers and investors, all of whom want to find ways to tap into this market place, reach those busy users and find ways to capture and influence some share of their activity. And if Facebook is considered too broad a market place, then there are other sites with more niche audiences such as: Foursquare with its mobile location-based networking service; Groupon, which offers group-wide deals and discounts, a form of "social shopping"; Twitter; Pandora (which has a partnership with Facebook but is an independent company offering free internet radio, enabling the sharing of music and radio selections); Academia (social networking for academics and those in education and research); OneClimate for those concerned about climate change; FriendsReunited, one of the first SM places for old school pals to reconnect... In fact, a recent listing on Wikipedia shows at least 200 SM sites, all targeted at different groups and communities across the world. And there are more being launched.

If a site can truly "own" a sizeable network of dedicated inter-communicators, the potential of SM is so enormous that not just Private Equity but also the big investment banks are circling, looking for ways to exploit this. Goldman Sachs and Morgan Stanley have, for example, allegedly both been stalking Groupon. It sounds almost like there's another internet bubble building, with huge valuations being talked about. Groupon was only founded in 2008 by Andrew Mason who raised $1m from a few friends. Just two years later it rejected a $6bn bid from Google and the following year it was being talked about as potentially the largest Tech IPO ever! Pandora, slightly more modestly, is being talked about in terms of a possible $100 million IPO and at least it can claim some 10 years of continued site-building and investment and some 75 million registered users. With Facebook setting the bar at 2011 valuations of some $50bn on revenues of just $2bn, there is for the moment no limit on what these SM ventures could be worth.

Of course, the justification for such valuations is all based on the long term. These major SM sites are staking out the future ground and are developing such a Brand name and franchise that it's hard right now to see them ever being supplanted. Even as technology evolves, these SM leaders can be expected to have the cash, the investors and the partnerships that will see them able to adapt and change and stay one step ahead.

Why has Facebook so far outstripped all the other players? Why did early winners like MySpace and FriendsReunited fall by the wayside and lose popularity and audience? What drives continued success? We can answer this by identifying three defining and at the time mould-breaking characteristics:

1   Facebook decided right from its early days to build an "ecosystem". They have gone to great lengths to enable the developer community to participate and to help create the whole Facebook experience. While others looked at adding new functionality or expanding into new geographies (MySpace being a good example), Facebook was establishing a platform which allows anyone to build social applications.

   The Platform provides a set of APIs and tools which enable 3rd party developers to integrate with the "open graph" — whether through applications on Facebook.com or external websites and devices. It has evolved from enabling development just on Facebook.com to one which also supports integration across the web and different devices:

▷ More than one million developers and entrepreneurs from more than 180 countries.
▷ More than 550,000 active applications currently on Facebook Platform.
▷ Every month, more than 70% of Facebook users engage with Platform applications.
▷ More than 250,000 websites have integrated with Facebook Platform.
▷ More than 100 million Facebook users engage with Facebook on external websites every month.
▷ The Facebook platform now has a substantial library of documentation and guidelines.

Facebook Developer Platform

Data Store API Documentation

Documentation on data store API and the functions of the Data Store API (Specialized Tables, Distributed Tables, and Associations)
http://wiki.developers.facebook.com/index.php/api

Facebook Markup Language (FBML)

Introduces the Facebook Markup Language (FBML). Includes valid HTML elements, Facebook tags (e.g. user/groups, profile-specific and tools), dynamic FBML attributes, usage notes, invalid CSS attibutes and more.
http://wiki.developers.facebook.com/index.php/FBML

Links to Developer Documentation

Provides links to outsider developer platform resources. Includes tutorials from Microsoft, udPics, Tucows and more. Discusses updating apps with user-specific data, an introduction to Facebook Markup Language (FBML), Facebook photo uploads, PHP pagination for Facebook, applications and guides to getting started with Facebook application development.
http://wiki.developers.facebook.com/index.php/
Links_to_relevant_developer_docs

This initiative is clearly substantial and there are a large number of blogs and discussion forums, both sponsored by Facebook and many others independently established where there is constant dialogue and exchange of process and method for establishing Facebook connections. No other major SM site (and outside of SM only Apple and perhaps Amazon can truly compare) has come close to encouraging this depth and breadth of user and follower activity. As Mark Zuckerberg, the founder, has said: "Let us build the social web together."

2 Despite this huge wave of development and growth, Facebook's look and feel, its "user-interface" has not become cluttered and distracting to site users. The surge in applications and number of visits could have spoiled the whole experience but Facebook have managed to find a balance – navigation has remained simple and the essential user experience has changed little since its early days. In addition, advertising, which is the basic revenue model and value justification, has been encouraged but is well-integrated. There is a series of targeted and contextually relevant advertising guidelines which are reinforced by users themselves who are quick to deride any advertising which is overtly intrusive.

3   Brands have been actively encouraged to get involved. They can essentially tap into the Facebook world and critically can do so at little or no cost. And the long-term upside for Facebook is that brands will become increasingly tied and dependent on the FB channel. They will drive activity, usage and further visitor activity which will in turn drive up the ad rates that FB can charge. To date, while a number of high profile brands have set up Facebook pages, their presence amounts to only about 2 million pages so they represent still only a relatively small proportion of the total number of brands and companies that could participate. Expect that number to grow rapidly through 2011 and 2012 as having a Facebook page becomes as essential as having your own website. As one ad agency has described it: "We speak to companies every day who are interested in developing their social media strategies. When they are presented with the facts and potential benefits nearly all those companies decide to implement a social media plan."

As a sign of this rate of progress, Facebook is expected to double ad revenue in 2011 to close to $4bn. That is part of the near-70% increase in SM advertising spend that is forecast by eMarketer for 2011, pushing total global ad spend on SM networks to $7bn. SM's share of total online spend in the US in 2011 is expected to be around 10%. That is likely to increase substantially as social networking becomes more and more integrated in everyday commerce and communications.

Fundamentally we are seeing a complete shift in marketing and advertising communications and perhaps the biggest revolution ever in this sector. It's historically always been dominated by "push". The main idea used to be that a brand would develop its strategy and plan. The brand would take the lead and do all the work. It would also often use mostly "push"-type media like TV, radio and print which, despite all the media owner blurb about targeted communications, are essentially mass broadcast media which are received casually and often passively by the consumer. "Below the line" marketing such as direct mail did offer a more targeted audience reach but it's still brand ad push activity.

Now social networking comes along and we're beginning to see a "paradigm shift". It's starting to become less about what the brand pushes and much more about consumer "pull" – about what the consumer decides to look at, about their views and ideas and perceptions and how *they* choose to communicate it. David Jones, the Havas global CEO, describes this shift: "The relationship between advertisers and consumers is no longer linear." In his view consumers have become "prosumers" who have the power to make or break a brand. They decide whether to become brand advocates or not. If they don't like something, they have now their own reach and influence. They can bring a company down. The ad industry has shifted from "bought" media to "earned" media.

This shift is only gradually being recognized by brands, advertisers and their agencies. Agencies especially have been slow to adapt as they are wedded to their existing business model. As one industry chief said to me: "Last year we made 300 TV commercials, this year we'll do about the same. We know how to do that and we make good money doing it. It's all very well to talk about the internet and social media but that's historically not our skill set and we certainly can't reskill an entire office work force to suddenly become new media experts. So in the future the only way we can respond is to acquire another agency and hope that in the meantime our traditional stuff does not decline too rapidly"!

Meantime, new niche agencies that do have the know-how are emerging all the time. They are led by the generation who are growing up with this online and digital tech world and have understanding and the instinct to develop brand engagement plans that may never require the expense of mass broadcast TV in order to create a winning strategy. Here are some examples:

▷ *Ants Eye View* "concentrate on helping companies of all sizes understand and engage in customer collaboration, social media and community building." Clients include Apple, Microsoft, Cisco and Dr Pepper.

▷ *The Conversation Group* "is a global consultancy broadly dedicated to the art, science, and practical application of social technologies. We're enabling organizations around the world to radically scale their ability to discover, engage and collaborate with their constituencies, both inside and outside the enterprise."

▷ *Carrot Creative* "is a new-media marketing agency specializing in social media."

▷ *Social Media Group* is a large global social media shop. Clients include Ford, SAP and Yamaha.

▷ *Shift Communications* "is a fast-growing agency that lives at the intersection of influencer relations and social media."

▷ *1000 Heads*: "We're the Word of Mouth People. We make brand engagement an adventure that people want to talk about. We facilitate relationships that drive loyalty and sales."

These companies talk a different language. They are staffed and headed up by a different generation of leadership. In these early days they are all relatively small and agile and entrepreneurial and opportunistic and driven to do things differently. They are avid and active users and are themselves active bloggers and tweeters and Facebook fans. They experience this new media world and know more intuitively what will work and what will not. They represent a stark contrast to the some of the old dinosaur agencies.

They are engaging with the more enterprising brands and helping them to migrate from "push to pull", from "owned to earned", from old ways of engaging with their customers to a model fit for 2020:

▷ Alison Wightman, the marketing chief at Virgin Atlantic, reached out to social agency Qubemedia, to conduct a "Brand Sociability Review". Although already heavily engaged in grass-roots social networking, Virgin wanted a thorough check on what competitors were up to, what new lessons there were to be learnt and how to make sure they budgeted and spent appropriately.

▷ "Argos improve the entire business by listening to customers," ran a recent headline. What had Argos been doing? They decided to listen to what their customers were saying about them online and to use that channel to learn and engage. A key step was to add a high-profile customer-review feature to their website. Sounds straightforward enough, but the difference this time around was that the Argos team have collectively decided that they will look for that customer input to be the key driver of their own decision-making.

It wasn't easy for Argos to change from their usual way of doing business, which was by making decisions in large and long internal meetings. If they were to be serious about using social and consumer input then they had to get comfortable with fully allowing that. Many were worried about a lot of negative comment from consumers in social networks coming through and what they would do if that happened. "What will they say, how do we control what is said, should we try to control?"

In fact once the customer input process was underway, Argos found to their relief that most of the comments were positive. More than 500,000 reviews were received through 2010 and more than a million shoppers read the reviews on the site each week. So what consumers said was going to be very influential.

One year into the process they are all much more comfortable and confident about letting the consumer have this influence and control. The value of the negative in fact outweighs the value of the positive. "We listen to, and really understand, our customers."

Argos has meantime continued to evolve its social media program:

– Each week they contact over 1000 customers as a result of their ideas and comments. Customers often comment that they are surprised to hear back from the company.
– Reviews about product issues or faults are automatically collected and investigated.
– Buyers share the product feedback on a regular basis with manufacturers to improve quality and reliability. Customer ratings (a five-star system is used) are shared and improvements are targeted and measured. Trade and buying terms are influenced by this too.

– Product selection is driven by the customer feedback process, what is liked and what is not and most importantly what people want. That may simply be a different product color or size, more or less packaging and protection, or they may vote for a rival brand or just better availability.

Argos view this as part of their journey to adapt themselves to the changing world. If there's one message to emphasize, it is that they did take some 12 months to decide to do this. They realized that they could either just pay lip service to this way of operating or they could make a sea-change in the way they ran things. Naturally there were different views around the table but, coming up to 18 months on, there was no desire to go back to the old ways.

Argos had engaged leading media agency Mindshare and, as their business head Joanna Lyall says, "This is just the start of social media for Argos. We're looking at Twitter campaigns, blogger outreach and potentially YouTube. It's about how social media can change the business. Online community influence can also impact product offers and pricing models … the power of community could change the price consumers are willing to pay. It's not just a marketing tool but a way of doing business."

▷ American department store JC Penney has launched an integrated e-commerce site within Facebook that allows customers to buy its products without leaving the social networking site.

Customers of JC Penney, which has 1.3 million registered Facebook fans, will be able to post comments and recommendations to their friends when they visit the online store. The JC Penney Facebook page now has a "shop" tab that allows customers to browse through 11 departments, ranging from women's wear to jewelry, and place selections in their "shopping baskets".

Each product page features an image of the product, a short description, a Share button that allows users to post comments on their wall, and a Like button. The application is linked to Google Analytics, to enable JC Penney to analyze its return on investment by tracking campaigns, page metrics and conversions.

Other companies have created links to Facebook from their online stores which allow customers to share images with friends in the hope this will boost further sales, but this is the first time that a major retailer has created a complete store within the site. Other stores, such as American electronics retailer Best Buy, display their inventory on Facebook, but direct users to their own sites to complete transactions.

The extraordinary thing about these initiatives from Virgin, Argos and JCP is that they showcase a further stage in this shift from "push to pull". It used to be all about driving people to visit your website: "Come to us!" But now it's less and less about that. That key idea and principle is already being supplanted. And it's social networking that's causing the change.

There's been a huge investment in the last decade in encouraging people to visit the brand, type in the url, conduct a search on Google, Bing or elsewhere. But now brand marketers are recognizing that they need to go instead to their customers. They need to reach out and make contact *where* their customers are already, at the places online that their customers would naturally want to visit. They need to understand where those places are and engage *there*. Spending a lot of money and effort trying to persuade people to visit you is likely to be more expensive and will have a lower response rate. If a brand can engage with its customers in what for them is their natural home environment, then how much more effective can that be?

Drinks company Diageo recently revealed its future multi-channel marketing plans to scale back investment in their brand websites, starting with Bacardi, and to refocus marketing efforts on social media platforms that could host or contain their branded content. Diageo were experiencing a fall in visitors to their own sites which were not generating a return on investment. An article about this in the trade mag *NMA* commented that Bacardi expect to shift up to 90% of their digital spend to social media over the next two years "and most of that on Facebook".

This is an extraordinary development and we can certainly expect many other leading brands to follow suit and influence what others do. It is a powerful acknowledgment of the "paradigm shift" in advertising that is taking place and the power of communities and social media and being where your customers already are. And this starts to turn Facebook into a giant dominating community arena that every brand wants to play in. Perhaps this is why it's already being valued north of $50bn?

Does all this mean the end of brand websites and the death of Google? For sure, brands will still need to have their own home and will still need to make that a rich, engaging and reinforcing brand experience. And people will always want to be browsing and surfing and exploring and discovering and checking out things and using search engines to do that. But, nevertheless, what the JC Penney and Bacardi and others brand actions are showing is just how powerful social media, and Facebook especially, have become. SM will become the new "home" for all brands. Just as brands are going to need to configure their web presence for e-commerce and for m-commerce, they are now going to have to look at social or s-commerce as well. It's getting to be complex and demanding and is going to require exceptional determination and commitment to navigate a way through all these channels of opportunity.

Steve Robinson, who is the founder of online sports and clothing site MandMDirect, has coined the phrase "omni-commerce" or "o-commerce" and success is certainly going to require a very comprehensive multi-channel "omni-commerce" mindset!

JC Penney is not alone now in setting up these in-store SM stores. Asos.com, a UK online clothing store which has proved exceptionally popular, has announced that it too is setting up a store in Facebook. Asos claims that it will be the first retailer in Europe to do this. But with 11 million visitors a month and some 400,000 Facebook followers, the company feels it already has sufficient interest to make such an investment. It's intended that this store will have the same functionality as the website, including a full checkout experience. It will be adding a "like" function and the ability to share items and purchases with friends. Items that are listed by users will also appear in friends' newsfeeds which will provide the capability to click through to the Facebook store. Asos say that they have tested this move with customers before making the investment: millions of people who visit the website also interact with Asos on Facebook, commenting and sharing, and discovering new items. Many then go to the website to shop, so the Facebook store just makes this whole process quicker and easier.

One concern being raised is the role of Facebook itself in all this. At present it has not sought any sales commission. But it is very directly becoming a key intermediary and distributor. And brands like JC Penney and Asos are leveraging the huge volumes of Facebook traffic. These are very early days and sales through these "in-store" websites is still small. But if that changes and say 20%/30%/40% of JC Penney online sales start coming through Facebook, then for sure someone in Facebook will be asking the very obvious question: Shouldn't we be finding some way to get some of that value?

As shown in Figure 6 overleaf, social commerce very much has the potential to sit centre stage and become a commanding way for brands to do business online.

The idea of "social shopping" provides an added dimension to shopping online. For those who just want to click and buy it will be of little interest. But many want something more. Research from IMRG shows that 61% of people (and more women than men) enjoy shopping – it's a major form of relaxation and they especially like the social side of it.

They like the idea of shopping with friends and the potential of being able to replicate that experience in an online environment is very attractive. So, for example, Asos.com already appeals because it offers a "hub for fashionistas". Over 1.7million people have profiles on the Asos "Life" section of their website where they can and do post reviews and views, read blogs, join select fashion groups and in particular give and get style and fashion ideas. It gives the whole experience of shopping at Asos a warm and engaging feel and enables people to in effect "shop with their friends". They can set up

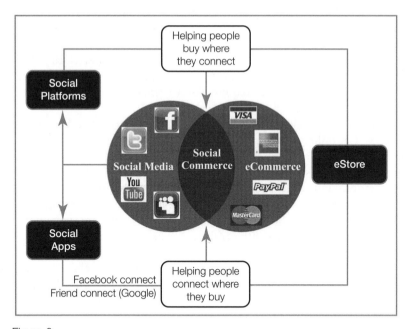

Figure 6
Source: theCustomerCollective

their "wish list" or just message friends or everyone to ask for opinions on a particular item of clothing.

An early pioneer in this was MyFaveShop.com which established the idea of co-browsing. A shopper could arrange with a friend to go online together, one evening at 7pm, say, to look for a "present for Mum". A simple software download or link, for example, now available from Ginza or BrowsePal enables friends to look at the same screen and follow one person's click journey as they explore various options. Ally this to a webcam and/or instant messaging and you have a real-time co-shopping experience which can bring friends and family together from all over the world

Another way to encourage this "social shopping" which is gaining a lot of interest is called "Social sign-on". This enables site visitors to log-in using their social media log-in credentials, such as Facebook, Twitter, Yahoo and others, rather than having to register separately on a new site or remember another set of user name and password access details.

For an e-commerce operator, this development is very attractive because it makes it much easier and quicker for people to get busy on their site and to get engaged with the product and content displayed. It also gives the site the personal data of whoever has logged in and, for example, their Facebook details, so there is an immediate benefit in adding to their database without the need to ask visitors to fill in tedious registration forms.

It is likely that "social sign-in" will become ubiquitous. And why not? It's just a simple and convenient alternative which visitors can choose to use. A survey by Gigya showed that c.18% of content publishers and retailers had already implemented this feature by end of 2010 and that as many as 50% said they had plans to introduce it during 2011. All those surveyed acknowledged that it would likely "improve engagement with their customers" and "provide a richer profile for subsequent targeting of product information, promotions and coupons." Jeff Grau, who conducted the survey, reckons that: "Once consumers give a retailer permission to access their personal data on Facebook, then their profiles and their likes will give valuable insight on what their visitors are interested in. They are the 'Alpha shoppers' because they are more likely to comment, provide feedback, share and review and provide insight."

All this is a further stage towards establishing the big social media networks as the key intermediaries and distributors of the 21st century. In former times, if a brand wanted to build its business it would worry about Wal-Mart or Target or Tesco and building relationships with those large-scale organizations. But these organizations are becoming less dominant in this growing multi-channel world. There are others which are now taking more and more distributor share. And as mentioned, they've yet to flex that leverage and traffic power!

Brands cannot afford not to get involved. It's no longer enough to "dip a toe in the water" and to explore this world a bit further. An increasing number of brands are reporting significant increases in site traffic and in many cases also increasing sales if they engage with SM networks. For example, LoveFilm, ESPN and IGN.com have found that integrating Facebook Open Graph functionality has "significantly extended" the brand. IGN, the gaming and entertainment site which already had some 29m users a month, said traffic was up 20% in the month after integration. ESPN reported a similar effect: "It's not just the increase in visitors, we've also seen that they spend more time on our site." LoveFilm said that they had experienced a 300% increase in traffic: "Many are now getting involved in 'liking' movies and actors and that feature has suddenly grown in prominence as it's being actively shared."

All brands now need a clear and long-term strategy and plan about how to fully capture the share of voice and opportunity that the social networks bring. The main strategic options are:

1. Listen and Monitor
2. Establish a community
3. Promote product and services
4. Extend brand franchise with engaging content
5. Sell product /services

It's quite feasible to start with option 1 and gradually add on the other components as the knowledge grows about how to make things work. Jumping straight in and starting selling might seem like fun but without all the other elements available it is high risk. The ability to monitor reactions and learn – to see what's working and what is not – will be crucial in building any kind of sustainable platform for success.

For many brands, that learning environment is best experienced on social chat networks where they can prompt a conversation about themselves and in a low profile way start to gather that "social intelligence." A network site like MumsNet is a good place to start. It has become a high profile place for Mums especially to network, share and comment. It's even had an influence on political elections when party leaders felt compelled to participate in the open chat forum on the site to answer questions, reassure the party faithful, address the opposition and try to gain support for policies. Gordon Brown, the former British Prime Minister hailed MumsNet as "one of the great British institutions", which is quite something for a site that has only been active for about 8 years.

The success of MumsNet is not in absolute number of visitors – that's just over a million uniques a month, so this will never be another Facebook – but the site is testimony to the power and influence of mothers everywhere and the far reach of their views. What is talked about and excites comment on MumsNet is actively monitored by all the main newspaper and consumer content sites. And they will pick up on discussion threads and quickly blow up what mums are talking about into national news. The site has become a key agenda setter and influence at both an individual product and company level as well as being a high profile voice in the broader debates of the day.

If a product is rated highly on MumsNet then conversion rates and sales go sky-high. Click-throughs to highly-rated product sites can often go up by as much as 20%, and 80% of mums say they rely on community feedback when deciding what to buy (MumsNet research). Microsoft Advertising research found that 63% of all mums interviewed went actively online for advice and tips on bringing up their family and on relationships, and to share likes, dislikes, favorites and ideas. 99% of active mums in the survey said that they typically logged in at weekends or late evenings and an increasing number were using their smart phone for convenient access. As Hilary Graves of niche children's food brand Little Dish has commented: "Most mothers agree the best source of information to shape their purchase decision is other mums … but as a brand owner you can only achieve so much by relying on people finding you online. Mummy bloggers allow a brand to spread the word far wider, and for that brand to be taken more seriously. It's a great way to generate exposure." A rival site to MumsNet is called iVillage, and their business head Lulu Phongmany has highlighted the power of this mums' network: "It's one thing for a brand to have a Facebook page … but conversations on branded message boards are longer and more involved." "One advantage [for brands working with aggregated content portals such as iVillage] is the tacit endorsement that association with a trusted portal gives them."

For brands trying to influence what's being said about them it's a challenging time and it's already become clear that any participation or overt and explicit communication on a social network needs to be very carefully managed. It can often be perceived as a brand "barging in" on, for example, any negative comment in which they have been mentioned. "It is like interrupting someone else's conversation." And it can backfire. Research has shown that even mentioning a customer service call centre number can provoke intense irritation and derision as customers vent their anger at the typical costs, frustrations and delays of trying to get satisfaction from a call centre

Lulu Phongmany of iVillage suggests that you should not be afraid of criticism. It is much better to take the stance of "OK, we'll take that on board and we'll change it and we'll let you know when we've changed it." Brands such as Dell have been pioneers in how to get this interaction right. They were early monitors and participators in social forums and did start barging into every conversation. But they quickly learned to turn people who disliked their product into positive advocates. They asked for more detail, they listened, they promised to make changes … and they did. The negatives got turned into positives. Dell saw the power of establishing a community of brand enthusiasts as well as industry watchers whose blogs received a wider following and who were influential. They invited them to visit the factory, they gave them pre-launch product to test, they invited them to certain events, they offered exclusive items for sale and have substantially extended a global fan base. It's also led to more sales, with Dell claiming that some incremental $25m of additional sales in 2010 were directly attributable to their social networking.

Here's what some other brands are doing to leverage the SM world. They are pioneering the new forms of marketing and establishing the trends for SM effectiveness:

▷ Ford provided free use of its new Galaxy people carrier model for a month to a group of mums who'd been especially vocal, blogging and mailing on MumsNet about rival car models and how they compared. The only "ask" was that the mums would video their experiences with the car for subsequent showing on MumsNet and YouTube. The mums were given a free video camera as well! "It was great for us as we got some really useful feedback and the honest and genuine testimony from the mothers provided some real substance and facts about the Galaxy and who it would be best suited for."

▷ EA Games has worked to take advantage of the Facebook "places" function which allows users to "check-in" or just update their status with their location information. EA has introduced a series of competitions which only users who had checked in at one of their tour events could enter. The prizes were of course free games and the competition proved to be very successful. It attracted large numbers of people to physical locations where they could experience the games. It helped promote the EA brand to the entire friend list of anyone who checked in. It had a knock-on effect as EA noted a sales boost at stores near the event during the following week. "We expanded

Source: EA Games

our fan base, generated a lot of online impressions and actually our marketing spend via Facebook was very little."

▷ Blackberry's strategy is to use Facebook as one of their key brand-building tools. They actively encourage people to visit their page and then make a lot of effort to keep them there without being navigated away. This is an important factor in designing a brand's SM presence because users are bombarded by constant distractions such as ads, notifications, updates and messages. "We want the user to find value on the page and consider returning to the page if not purchasing a product or service listed. If the page holds sufficient value then the visitor will 'like' the page. Our

Source: RIM BlackBerry Brodeur Partners

goal is to provide constantly updated information with a few quick ideas and incentives."

Blackberry encourages Wall posts and discussion about its products, includes video, competitions, links and notes, product info, offers to find local fans near you and has a running total, growing all the time, of the number of its Facebook fans worldwide: "Join *our* community!"

▷ Marmite, the food spread, represents a good illustration of a "joint venture". Rather than trying to be social media experts themselves this Unilever brand co-opted an existing group of Marmite fans. This group had already set up their own unofficial Marmite fan page on Facebook and been gathering interest and fans for three years. Unilever decided to invite 30 Marmite lovers recruited from the fans network to a "secret briefing" before the launch of the new Marmite XO. They were asked to participate in a blind tasting for the three shortlisted product variants. And they were actively involved in deciding which one Unilever should go with. These "core" fans were then asked to spread the word (as well as the product). The campaign broke new ground for Unilever. It proved to be an effective model for product testing by getting the initial buzz in the market. Co-creation establishes interest and demand which makes a difference to the success of the launch, and Unilever plan to include it in future research plans and innovation efforts.

This type of approach is being dubbed the "IKEA effect", where consumers are variously encouraged, enabled or persuaded to invest *their* energy and time into a product. In IKEA's case, in putting it together! It is proving a powerful way to create a greater sense of ownership among the target customer and user base. They are more likely to feel responsible for its success and, as the various case studies demonstrate, their testimony, comments and advocacy can be far more potent than $m spent on TV advertising. Burberry has been down this path with its "Art of the Trench" where consumers submitted photos of themselves wearing the famous coat with a view to their becoming the "face of the brand". Burberry then selected people, changing the face on a regular basis but promoting each person as one of its style leaders and models. Nike ID is a now well-established route for consumers to style their own shoe and that by itself has created a very profitable revenue stream. And Threadless.com allows consumers to post their own t-shirt designs. The community votes on the best ones, which are then created and offered for sale. "This simple idea generates a lot of traffic to our site."

With all these case studies and examples, using social media as a core part of a brand's communication strategy should be obvious. But many brands, agencies and marketers have yet to take this step. Studies by the IAB and Retail Research Centre found that over one-third of brands in early 2011 had no policy on social media at all. They found a lot of confusion about how social media fits into a business strategy with many companies struggling to know what to do and where to start. Most still see it as a PR tool and the most common initiative is to establish a Facebook page but without any plan about what to do with it. There have been a number of poor executions which can result in anything from being simply a drain on company resources with no benefit for the business or its customers to more serious repercussions such as damaging the brand image.

So in summary what are the key lessons and how should a brand go about taking advantage of this arena. There are seven keys:

1 *Do not treat SM networks as direct sales channels.* They are not. Overt selling may simply upset and irritate.
2 *Treat the interaction as "social".* The focus should be on talking directly and personally to customers, strengthening relationships and most importantly building loyalty.

    There may be some short-term sales benefits to be had by promoting new products and offering immediate incentives. But such activities just need to be promoted in a way that suits the channel.
3 *Be a good listener.* The general rule of thumb in social networking is to spend around 70% to 80% of the time in listening and responding and 20% to 30% in proactively communicating your own messages – just enough to spark interest.
4 *Ask good questions.* For example, the Marmite social media plan started with a simple question: "We're thinking of launching a new version of Marmite, what do you think about that?"

5 *Give people a reason to get engaged.* This means having a key content plan and strategy that needs to be invested in, constantly updated and regularly (could be every day) adjusted and changed. It needs to be compelling enough that a visitor will stick around. As usual, first impressions count. What users see when they visit will totally determine their relationship with you. If it's poor they won't come back, customer lost. If it's good, you start to tap into the value of social advocacy.

6 *Make some stuff exclusive.* Make the most interesting and desired content available only to fans. And make it easy to become one. It won't take much to convert a page hit into a "like". Once you've got that "like", you've opened up a direct channel of communication with that person. And all their online friends will see this interest and that can drive more traffic towards your brand.

7 *Test and trial ways to convert the fan base into a customer base.* If it's too pushy you'll be told very quickly. But your Facebook fans will not be unfamiliar with some degree of brand push and will tolerate it. Blackberry used their Facebook pages to push their Playbook, but it was done by way of information – product news, pictures, specs etc. – first before, for example, competitions and incentives to win or buy one.

Marketers can also easily measure and monitor how well their efforts are doing. What is working and what is not. What is the business case for doing more in this area? How do we justify diverting precious resource and budget away from more traditional approaches? How do we move to a position where we can start getting this multi-channel communication really working? How do we learn how to take advantage of the shift from "brand push" to "consumer pull"? There are some straightforward and "measurable metrics":

▷ Social Media views: the number of views of the social media content, e.g. views of your Facebook page, YouTube channel, blog etc.
▷ Fans and Followers: how many and the trend.
▷ Likes, Retweets and Shares: the number of actions taken to forward or recommend content to others.
▷ Traffic: the amount of traffic your website gets from social media networks.
▷ Sales and Conversions: the amount that can be attributed to social media activity. Analytic packages can follow the site visitor journey from SM networks just as affiliates can track clicks from search engines.
▷ PR: as a contributor to brand-building, traditional measures of column inches and type of content.
▷ Market research trends: establish a benchmark of consumer attitudes and brand ratings and measure over time the changes to that.
▷ Loyalty: measure repeat purchase levels from the existing customer base and where those customers came from (e.g. Zappos claim Twitter is a major generator of customer leads and has led to 75% of orders coming from repeat customers).

This area has such a high level of interest that there has been a rush of software tools and agencies all offering to create dashboards that will record these various metrics and report on trends and progress. We looked specifically at a 6 step test and brand check in Chapter 5. However, other companies like BuzzCapture, ViralHeat, SAS Media Metrics, MarketWire, Sentiment Metrics and a score of others all offer various approaches that means there's no reason at all for a brand not to be able to learn how to make this social media world work for them.

And finally, while most of our examples have been about the dominance of Facebook with its 600 million plus registered users and fans, Twitter sits alongside as the other key social networking location. See Plate 5.

There are many examples of brands who have found that Tweeting is more productive than Facebook paging. JetBlue has been active on Twitter for 3 years and learnt that customer service updates lent themselves well to the short messaging format. Letting people know about general flight information, airport access, weather delays generated large numbers of tweets and retweets. And because JetBlue was an early pioneer it has generated for itself a lot of positive PR. Another example, Etsy, is an online market place for buying and selling all things handmade. They found that people were using Twitter to promote items for sale to friends and colleagues so they have used Twitter to tap into this. They let followers know about particularly innovative products and alert people to offers and promotions. "We find it's a valuable way to harness the creative minds of the community." Consider also Naked Pizza, which is a growing chain of US pizza restaurants that has found Twitter to be its key marketing tool. "We have a built a strong customer base around healthy eating and it's been very cost effective." In fact it's working so well that kiosks are being set up in-store where customers can sign up for a Twitter account and on the website there is a Naked Pizza Twitter stream to showcase what people are saying about the pizzas. In their last survey, they found that 68% of total sales came from customers who said "I'm calling from Twitter."

Perhaps the final word on this social media phenomenon should be from Stephen Fry who has become one of the world's most celebrated Tweeters or Twitterers (people remain divided about the "right" term). "People are not just business people or consumers, they are just people. We are made as emotional characters and if we want to interact with others we want that to be joyful. Social media needs to be led by a human understanding first and a business understanding second. If businesses lead with their wallets and not their hearts they will fall by the wayside with social media. Exploiting your followers for commercial gain is not the way. Keep them updated. Keep them informed. Share ideas and news. Build trust. Have fun! Be exciting! Listen to what people are saying. All of us have a voice and now we can be heard."

9 Social TV

Social Media is becoming a fundamental part of our lives but it's about to get even more mainstream. It's going to appear on a TV near you any time soon. "Social TV" is already being touted as the next bit game changer waiting to revolutionize our lives. Still waiting to get that flat screen TV, looking enviously at HDTV and the crystal clear display, imagining what it would be like to have 3D in the living room, budgeting to access movies on demand via NetFlix or LoveFilm … already seeing a whole horizon of gradually upgrading your TV watching habits? Well, even while consumers are getting up to speed with all these innovations, the next generation of TVs is already in production and being shipped.

Variously called Web TVs, "connected" TVs or "internet-enabled" TVs, here is another attempt at device convergence whereby your TV also becomes your internet screen giving you access to the Net while also giving you TV, VOD/movies and the easy ability to socialize while doing all these things. And while there have been attempts in the past to achieve this screen convergence from "multi-screen" to one screen, this time it's going to happen because the big computer software and hardware players have got involved. Apple TV and Google TV are already well-advanced and available, and these two, alongside other applications from the likes of Samsung and Sony, are set to transform TV viewing in the future.

Why this interest and large-scale investment?

▷ A 2011 study from Thinkbox and Decipher showed that 92% of people in the survey used online for catch-up TV and programs that they would otherwise have missed. The main reason cited is "convenience".
▷ However, half of these people said they would prefer to watch catch-up TV on the TV rather than their PC.
▷ Intel research has shown that c. 45% of consumers use social networking sites to discuss TV programs such as *The X Factor* while that program is airing.
▷ 19% of consumers in the Thinkbox/Decipher survey said that they'd prefer to use a smart phone or other device to do their social networking – "easier than having to log on".
▷ More women than men chat online while watching TV.
▷ 74% of 18- to 24-year-olds regularly browse the Net while watching TV.

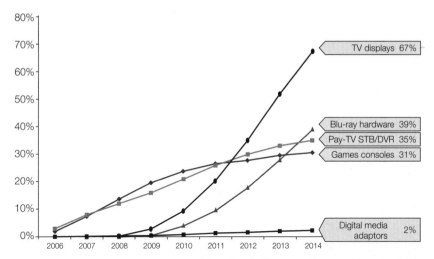

Figure 7   **Household saturation of IP-enabled devices, Western Europe, 2014**
Source: FutureSource Consulting Ltd

▷ 62% said they had emailed others and 61% said they generally browsed the
   web while TV watching.
▷ 52% said they had gone online to shop while watching a program and
   that they were looking to buy an item that was being featured on the TV
   program (the further rise of the multi-channel consumer!).
▷ And the key commentator on this sector, FutureSource, predicts a surge
   in this area and in the number of IP-enabled TVs (Figure 7).

Against this latent interest and demand, TV manufacturers are now in-
corporating internet access into their new generation of TVs (Plate 6). It's
expected that they will ship some 20 million "connected TVs" into Europe
during 2011. And by 2015 (according to FutureSource) 95% of all TV sales
will have this additional functionality. This will likely also mean that in the
US some one-third of all homes will have connected TVs installed. And what
will the consumer see? Typically there will be a "home page" interface with a
standard menu of options listing, for example:

TV		*Internet*
Catch-up TV		*Facebook*
Movies		*YouTube*
Music	*Source:* Philips	*Games*

What will distinguish this home page from other home page interfaces will be the addition of an apps list. Top of the tree is likely to be Facebook and Twitter, providing seamless quick access to social engagement. And then, like an iPad or Galaxy or Playbook, depending on your personal selection, you can download and populate various apps straight onto that home page as your key preferences, functions and utilities. Expect an "instant messaging" window where tweets and Facebook mails can be seen and read, an onscreen cursor/typepad or off-screen keyboard for short messaging, as well as a Skype video call window. It is forecast by GigaOM that 1 billion TV apps will

have been downloaded by 2015. (Compare that with the 10 billion Apple apps downloaded from the App Store by Jan 2011.) TV apps are expected to ramp up more slowly over the next few years as replacing the home TV happens on longer lead times, but once the market reaches critical mass it will surge to a new level.

"One screen convergence" in fact becomes a series of multi-windows integrated into one main screen and making the TV a wholly engaging, interactive and live experience. Russell Owens at Samsung explains that they want people to start thinking beyond just passively watching content, whether in catch-up form or a movie on demand. Here is an opportunity to see the TV box as the core home entertainment device and the idea is to provide different levels of activity and interaction around specific TV shows.

This will have appeal to a wide number of players in the value chain: TV manufacturers who will see a premium for their next generation sets; content producers who can develop spin-off sales and product merchandising (sophisticated forms of product placement); telcos and mobile phone operators who will have added access and opportunity to provide, for example, immediate voting for favorites and competitions; developers who will see another outlet for apps; games console manufacturers who can look to provide this one screen converged facility from their games console; and also brands and marketers who will have yet further choice and opportunity to reach out to their target audience and strengthen their brand franchise.

This new era in the role of the TV device will bring substantial challenges to existing TV channel operators. While they have some existing control through their brand name, distribution reach and general market presence, they have of course been struggling in recent years with declining audiences and advertising revenues. As broadband IP connectivity improves, it is possible to deliver broadcast-quality TV over the existing fixed infrastructure. At the same time, Ethernet connectivity and web service technology based on open standards are being incorporated into the TV or set-top box and this can create an "open TV" environment. That is very different from the early

Web 1.0 interactive TV "walled garden" which was pioneered by Sky TV in the UK. At that time the lack of good broadband, the clunky interface, the restricted content, the high level of charging for a brand to participate and the limits on content all inevitably restricted web TV's early development. In an open internet access world with today's much higher levels of bandwidth, these roadblocks and constraints have been removed. Now Sky TV must work to make its content as relevant for an internet TV generation and compete in the open market. Every player will want its brand to feature on the TV menu home page. Initially, the incumbent TV owners such as BBC, ITV, NBC etc. will dominate but new players will quickly capture share of that home page influence and territory.

Google TV is certainly one of the most advanced and ready-to-go solutions. It was launched in October 2010 and is a joint venture involving Intel, Sony and Logitech. It uses the Google Android operating system and the Google Chrome browser to create a "new experience for television". This will be incorporated directly into HD TV sets, into Sony Blu-ray players and into set-top boxes developed by Logitech, all using new Intel Atom chips. Google has also announced a partnership with NetFlix (amid rumors that they will also acquire that company) to give users access to the NetFlix library of movies and TV shows.

This "complete" market offering is distinctive because it is providing a globally standardized platform which can scale quickly and easily. It's likely to replace current VOD providers, especially in Europe where they have remained fragmented and parochial. For example, in France over 40% of households have VOD but there are nine different providers competing for share. In Germany, ownership of cable infrastructure is also fragmented and many platforms are based around one region only. With low market muscle and marketing from suppliers, VOD only has a c.5% market penetration and none is at critical mass to make an IPTV service economically viable. So, not only is existing competition limited but none have the profit base and reach of Google.

Google TV's own advertising neatly captures what it is setting out to do:

▷ "There's more on TV than television"

▷ "The web is now a channel"

▷ "A new world of apps for your TV"

▷ "Your phone = remote control"

▷ "Fling a video to your television"

▷ "Watch it now"

▷ "Watch and browse, simultaneously"

▷ "TV gets a homepage"

▷ "Record from the search bar"

Source: Samsung Electronics

Initial market reactions to Google TV were lukewarm, commenting on the still-early stages of this market initiative with the view that it is still for early adopters and technophiles (but they said that about the web in its early days too!). The user interface is still a bit clunky with a home page simply adapted from the web, using a small QWERTY keyboard that is shipped with the TV to type in and search for specific content. Users navigate by using search terms or browse using a program guide on the Google TV home screen. It does offer social media links.

Also not yet resolved at time of writing is access to all of TV. The likes of NBC, ABC, CBS, Viacom and Hulu had yet to reach agreement with Google on content access.

Nevertheless and undeterred, Google immediately opened up its development environment and site owners and content developers can start developing applications to work on the Google TV platform. Google have acknowledged that this is TV Web 1.0, so we can expect continued upgrade and development as learning and experience grow. For example, in 2011 Google quietly acquired Widevine, which provides "a better video delivery experience" and can also integrate with non-PC-based media such as mobile and works with a wide variety of smart phones, set top boxes and games consoles. Google is also said to be in partnership discussions with Vudu who specialize in "on demand instant streaming direct to the TV".

However, Google will not have it all their own way. Their major rival is likely to be Apple TV. Apple have not set up the series of major global partnerships that Google have and, while their reach is not so immediately scalable, they do score inevitably on the way their system looks – the design and the user interface.

It's a simple plug-and-play solution: plug the sleek set-top box into your TV and just click and play. It enables streaming of films, TV programs and photos and syncs up with an iTunes library. But it is not the open access environment found on Google TV. Apple, as they have always done, like to do it their way. So while there

Source: Apple

is wide-scale content access there is no open internet facility. The content sits within Apple's "walled garden" and has been criticized at one level for not doing much more than putting iTunes content plus YouTube onto your TV. The iPhone or iPad are enabled as remote controls and through them you can type your content search with the QWERTY keyboard and use the "remote" controls to play/fast forward etc.

A further constraint with Apple's solution here is that the TV program access is limited. At the time of launch in late 2010, the only TV networks who had signed up were BBC, ABC, Disney and Fox. And while Apple naturally say they are in negotiation with others we've yet to see any new partners on board. At the same time movie content can only be rented not purchased and Apple have provided no technical or commercial reason why. But at the end of the day this way of establishing a form of "connected TV" is just easy to use and is inexpensive, at only $99.

There are a number of other solutions and providers, all looking to capture a slice of this emerging area. Roku, a privately-held US company, has a set-top box on the market which provides video/movie streaming onto the TV. It also offers the facility of accessing the internet using your TV as the screen in the same way that games consoles from Nintendo, Sony and X-box have done for some time. Tivo has launched an iPad App which enables you to search, browse, explore and share content in one window while still watching a TV program on the main screen. Tivo brands this as a "true two-screen TV experience". Starling TV is scheduled to launch in 2011, offering social TV which will enable viewers to watch TV while watching Facebook and/or Twitter comments scrolling across the bottom of the screen (a different kind of news feed). Boxee is another US-based set-top box product, this one from start-up D-Link, which is intended to provide catch-up TV programming and movies direct to the TV. It operates somewhat like a Logitech box and provides open internet access to the TV screen alongside movies etc. It too comes with a remote and a QWERTY key pad. What distinguishes Boxee from the raft of other VOD set top boxes is its social TV features. Register an account and you can share and post videos you like, and link it to Facebook and Twitter to look at video content that your friends like. If Boxee is hooked into Facebook, for example, then all the videos your friends and you post will show up automatically. General internet access has, however, been criticized as being slow and clunky and so, while Boxee is attracting plenty of interest, it's not yet ready to become a major player in the open social TV arena.

In the meantime, a number of vanguard Brands and media owners are already looking to take early advantage of social TV:

▷ "Social TV goes Dutch" ran a recent EuroVision report. *The Voice of Holland* is a Dutch talent show which has started to give viewers the ability to rate what they're watching and how well they think a performer is doing in real time. A sliding bar appears on the screen which captures and shows viewers votes as they come in. Performers are stopped if the bar stays low for too long! This function first aired in January 2011 and is part of a new social TV platform in Holland called PlayToTV. The ratings are made on either Facebook or Twitter and also enable viewers to compare social data with their friends. Dutch TV News has been closely following this innovative format and it's already been picked by NBC in the US.

▷ Tesco has announced that it is working to let shoppers update their on-line shopping lists through their TVs. This is another experiment by this multi-national grocer to explore IPTV services in which it would send messages to its online customers, in the first instance mailing only those who use the Tesco own brand Technika Freeview set-top box. In 2009, Tesco looked at applications that were like a virtual fridge door where a family could post shopping lists as well as "to-do's", photos etc. That has not been progressed but reports suggest Tesco is committing much more this time around. Tesco's Head of Internet R&D, Nick Lansley says:

> We are playing with what's possible. If this works, we'll look at offering some transactions through the TV ... [and we] will look at expanding the trial [to] take it to the mass market. We might look at sponsoring a cookery show ... People could push a button on their remote to add ingredients being used on TV to their online basket.

To accelerate their developments in this area and also to provide a more immediate capability, Tesco have gone on to acquire an 80% holding in Blinkbox. Blinkbox has a strong technology platform for internet-connected TV content and programming and also offers movie rental and video streaming. "Working with the Blinkbox team we can bring more compelling product propositions to our customer base."

▷ Channel 4 in the UK has been experimenting with a form of social TV which marries live TV shows with online activity, although for the moment this takes place on separate screens. For the first time on UK TV, viewers at home can pit their wits against TV studio-based contestants, playing along with the live TV show *The Million Pound Drop.*

By tuning into www.channel4.com/drop TV viewers can "experience, first-hand, the excitement and tension of the live shows", taking part in the online game. Mirroring the main show, players of the online game are given a virtual £1m, then must try to keep as much of their cash as possible as they tackle the same questions in real-time as the TV contestants. Answers are made by placing a portion of their winnings over whichever trapdoors they believe holds the correct answer – a wrong answer will see the money swallowed through the trapdoor!

"The *Million Pound Drop* game offers a new level of interactive TV viewing, heightening the enjoyment, tension and drama of the live broad-cast," says James Bruce of the production company Pancentric. In addition the game show's host discusses live on-air how well the players of the online game are doing compared to the TV contestants. "As our show goes out live, the online game gives it a real event feel as thousands of online players answer every question. We've also integrated Twitter and Facebook into the website ensuring that once the live broadcast is under-way users can easily share their results and experiences with their friends and networks."

▷ The 2010 *X Factor* show attracted 11 tweets per second, the *Strictly Come Dancing* show had 7 tweets per second and the UK election debate between the party leaders got 29 tweets per second. Intel trends watcher David McKeown comments that, "It seems we are becoming a nation of armchair pundits, sitting watching TV with laptops at the ready so we can share our own commentary and opinions with friends and family whilst watching popular TV through social networks ... The rise of event TV is really fuelling this trend, especially prevalent for women ... This clearly demonstrates an appetite from consumers to have Internet connectivity whilst watching TV. Smart TV – a technological revolution will change the way we watch TV forever. It will not only become more interactive and responsive, but it will make TV an even more social experience."

▷ MediaCorp, operating in Singapore, is planning to launch through 2011 an interactive TV app via broadband, which enables you to book stock trades using the remote control. It's intended to capitalize on the very strong retail/consumer interest in market trading in the country. It's been trialed in Hong Kong and the company plan to roll this out into India as their next big market.

▷ ITV and Channel 4 in the UK are looking at micro-payment solutions so they can charge for individual items of content or programming. They foresee that as web TV enters the living room a new behavioral paradigm will emerge. Instead of viewers signing up for monthly packages they will cherry pick and choose only that content they prefer and pay "as they go". The TV companies are working with established micro-payment providers like Paypal and MPP to design solutions that will be easy to use and facilitate internet TV purchases.

As connected TVs get into more and more homes then "the early promise of the first generation of interactive TV is now finally able to be fulfilled." With the way that the technology has advanced, the combination of TV brand power plus the brand-enhancing interactivity will drive application and campaign development. It can lead viewers from simple passive entertainment to direct interaction with the TV to social TV with friends to content-related commerce and on to purchasing.

There will always be the familiar "red button" that puts you in touch with content that sits behind the 30 second ad and enables you to get more news, sport, weather and, for example, local information as well as dive deeper into program detail. This type of connection is widely used already by TV producers to deliver added value and has been used effectively in the past by the likes of Volvo and other car manufacturers to present more about their cars and enable viewers to select a brochure to be sent to their cable TV or satellite billing address. But now brands are starting to look at testing out specific and tailored e-commerce shopping facilities. That might start with an Amazon app which enables you to order a DVD of a movie that's being advertised or a book that's being discussed in a program. It could move to Tesco-type online shopping. How much easier would it be for parents at the end of the day to relax and watch the TV while in a separate window simply arranging for their regular weekly shop to be delivered at the usual time.

TV interaction will ultimately be governed by the nature of TV viewing. It is a "sit-back" generally passive and relaxing experience. For real web surfing and serious brand/product investigation, going direct to the website will still likely be the preferred option and that's mostly going to be through the PC and tablet, whether fixed line or wireless. But TV will still open up a wider world of possibilities for the true multi-channel operator.

As with any emerging new channel and communication medium there are teething problems and this will delay, but over the long term not prevent, brands from actively exploring this area. The two key technical roadblocks which will need to be overcome are (i) bandwidth and (ii) common technical standards.

(i) Improving bandwidth is crucial in order to enable seamless delivery of this rich media content IP connectivity, to allow easy and quick download of video, to allow immediate and quality internet access. And while most developed countries proudly talk about very high broadband penetration, the key is the line speed.

Japan boasts an average of 105 Mbps (megabytes per second) while the UK average is under best estimates no more than 4.5 and conservatively more like 1.5. Fiber optic cables to the home is the best means for delivering super fast connections and cable penetration into, for example, US households is more than 40% and into Japan it's high, at around 55%. But UK cable only reaches c.15% at best and it puts greater emphasis for the moment on ADSL (asymmetric digital subscriber lines) through the phone lines. While the phone line capability to handle data at speed has surpassed initial expectations, it does have a continuing number of quality issues. BT, the dominant fixed line telco provider in the UK, has talked up plans to lay a superfast cable network but that will not reach any degree of critical mass till 2015 at the earliest. Meanwhile Virgin Media through cable is already able to deliver up to c. 50 Mbps, but the high premium cost has limited uptake.

These line speed capabilities will not stop providers offering services and the likes of NetFlix and LoveFilm will undoubtedly significantly expand their customer bases for VOD. It won't stop Tesco experimenting with "bringing shopping into your living room" and it won't prevent the likes of MediaCorp rolling out their share trade services on TV. But it will influence the style of presentation, the ability to deliver in real time and the speed of the interaction.

(ii) A further potential roadblock is the absence of a common set of technical standards. While interactive and social TV is still in its early stages there are a variety of different platforms being deployed and this makes it a big challenge for the application developers to produce interactivity that has the widest possible reach. Certainly Google TV and Apple TV can be expected to vie with each other for market share and developer attention, and we may well see the kind of operating system competition that already prevails in the mobile market place. In the meantime, Samsung has set aside a "developer investment fund" to encourage developers to work with its platform and Sony too is looking at its own future options so as not to become totally dependent on Google.

Meantime the Digital TV Group (DTG) is trying to bring broadcasters, platform operators and consumer electronics manufacturers together into agreeing common standards. YouView (the major UK broadcaster iTV platform) is starting to put its weight behind DTG, hoping that by contributing and showing leadership then others will adopt its protocols and specifications. YouView is talking about an "open environment" for bringing the internet to TV, but it's likely that program makers, brands and advertisers will be asked to work within *its* guidelines. Because of their anticipated market power, especially for VOD and catch-up, they are already influencing behavior and all the main set manufacturers have indicated a desire to be "YouView"-compliant when that platform is ready to go live in 2011.

The CEO of DTG believes that in an ideal world, connected TV should be an ecosystem where all developers can easily develop and share. If that goal can be achieved then a much more scalable system can be established and companies will be able to manage down the costs of production. But opponents argue that healthy competition is essential to drive the necessary innovation and performance improvements that can make this medium a long-term success.

In sum, it's true to say that, like the old much-repeated adage: "Next year is going to be the year of the mobile," there have been forecasters foretelling the advent of interactive TV for a number of years. When the concept first hit our screens back in 1999, Sky TV in the UK were regarded as the global pioneers. They were doing it all themselves with a very local solution that relied on satellite broadcasting, dial up response, almost no broadband and so a very slow service, limited available functionality and a walled garden of content. Nevertheless broadcasters, content providers and program makers beat a path to their door. They wanted to learn because they realized the power and potential to make the TV come alive. Now, some 12 years later, technology has of course advanced many times and Facebook and Twitter have shown the power of easy chat and how so much of that can revolve around what's on TV. It is without doubt the way people will watch TV, it will be the norm by 2020 and probably widespread much earlier. Whether it's all on one TV screen, or TV plus laptop or TV plus laptop plus mobile, mobile as remote or a standard interactive remote, whether on Google or Apple or simply a net-connecting box which puts the internet on the TV screen, we will all be getting very used to much greater interaction with our TV sets.

10 Impact of Digital on Media, Travel, Health and Advertising

It is clear that we are witnessing a sea-change in the way business needs to operate. Technology innovation has combined with consumer demand and sophistication to produce a new order for successful commerce. No longer is it possible to operate successfully and sustainably using traditional approaches. The age has come for the multi-channel enterprise which is digitally savvy and embraces an "omni-commerce" approach to business. It requires a complete rethink about how to do business, how to engage with customers, how to organize in order to deliver that multi-channel engagement, how to stay abreast of the latest technology trends and decide what to focus on, and what to deprioritize. It means a new approach to sales and marketing, more informed decision-making about where and how to allocate budgets and new skills and training for the workforce to help them adapt and accept this changed landscape

And however challenging this changing world may appear to be today, we cannot expect that it will all calm down and that we will reach some plateau where slow-to-move businesses can finally catch up. Technology is on a rush and billions of dollars worldwide are being invested in new applications and developments. The open communities of software development pioneered by the likes of Apple are now the norm, enabling software to be enhanced, enriched and transformed by a global village of experts. This is happening at speed and it is no surprise that within 3 years some 300,000 applications had been launched for just one device, the Apple iPhone. Consumers live in a demanding environment where the developed world sees them as time-poor and searching greedily for convenience and ease. As a result, technology teams know that device innovation, service improvement, time saving and ease of access will quickly find commercial uptake and value

So businesses need to watch out! They need to be asking themselves just how much their organization understands the changes going on around them, how inculcated is that insight into the plans and strategies that the organization is pursuing and how advanced are they with their roadmap of adjusting and adapting and transforming themselves to this digital age?

There are five key questions that an organization could review to start examining its state of readiness and preparedness for this transformation journey.

1 Has there been any formal and wide-scale training and education about the new digital world and what its potential impacts will be? (The Chartered Institute of Management identified this area as the key training ground for the next 3 years.)

2 Do the current business plans reflect another year of incremental development or is there a strategy to test and trial new channels and ways of working? (Leading MCEs are spending c. 25% of their marketing budget in "new channels".)

3 Do people in the company regularly and at all levels talk about the impact of digital technology, about the need for transformation and about the multi-channel enterprise? (Leading MCEs identify this as a top-3 agenda item for 2011: "Discussion around multichannel retailing reached fever pitch ..." – *Retail Week*)

4 Is the company's investment and resource in social media at a token level or is it substantive? For example, is there a proactive and properly resourced (team of 2 to 3 per brand per country plus agency support) brand reputation monitoring and influencing program online?

5 Is the Technology department today actively adopting cloud computing, SOA, mobile connectivity, single view of the customer, real-time data analysis, online analytics? Are there projects which are looking enterprise-wide, for example, to implement a common and unified messaging and collaboration platform, a common and shared technical infrastructure? Is there an agreed vision for a next-5-year technical digital multi-channel architecture?

Transformation will come in all shapes and sizes. It can be enterprise-wide and of massive scale; it can be confined to one country or one business unit or a single function; it can start with a sweeping and new vision or it can begin with a few simple steps; it can be pioneering and adventurous; it can even be the stuff great case studies are made of; or it can be just a team that's determined to make a difference, that doesn't simply want to survive the next year or two on incremental tinkering but recognizes the need for far-reaching realignment to a world that's driven by technological advances which can provide new sources of competitive advantage.

To illustrate this, let's look at a number of different industries. We will examine which companies are in the vanguard and which are the laggards, who's making waves and who's just struggling to stay afloat, who will be the future winners, what are the lessons to be learnt for successful transformation and what are the potential strategic options.

The industries selected here provide a wide spectrum of different businesses. They are all consumer-facing or technology-based, *these* are sectors which are in the front line of change. They are the ones dealing every day with increased consumer and customer demand for ease and convenience and they are the ones most subjected to rapid advances in software and hardware development. B2B businesses outside that direct arena, such as investment banking/wholesale financial services, manufacturing and agriculture, are often one step removed from this onslaught of digital technology and may (no guarantee!), just may, have a bit more time to prepare their change program.

Travel

Let's first consider a sector where the transformation is already well under way. Travel was one of the first industries to experience online disintermediation. Airlines and hotel operators used to sell through travel bureaus and agents, and source most of their business that way. Reaching out direct was just not possible for cost and access reasons other than by, for example, direct mail drops which usually just led to an agent's call centre. But as we all know, digital technology has changed all that and now the traditional agents have either shut up shop, merged and consolidated or gone online themselves to capture the new order.

If we examine what's gone on we can see six different strategies that have been adopted:

(i)   *Hybrids*: companies as agents who now combine a mix of traditional retail as well as online travel booking such as STA Travel, Apollo and Co-op Travel in the UK.

(ii) *Forward integrators*: companies which have moved into other parts of the value chain, for example, Thomas Cook and Thompson which now have their own chartered airline services as well as providing holidays.

(iii) *Pure plays*: those which now focus exclusively on online direct, such as Cheapflights.com, Expedia.co.uk, LastMinute.com.

(iv) *Added value information providers* such as TripAdvisor.com.

(v)   *Segmented content/distribution plays* such as IgluSki.com.

(vi) *New low cost/adapted business model entrants* such as Trailfinders.com.

As we look into other sectors and explore the transformational changes that are just beginning to impact and are still far from complete, we can consider which of these possible strategies might be available and appropriate for incumbents and also for potential new entrants evaluating their options. That is not to say that the six strategic options identified here are the only ones that could be available. But they are a good place to start. They do all require a fundamental shift in ways of working, a wide-spread recognition and acceptance that the traditional model is on its last legs and a determination to go through often difficult change in order to safeguard the long-term health of the company. And of course, the current management may not be given much choice if rivals force the pace, if consumers demand change by buying elsewhere or if investors start selling!

Media

In the media sector, looking at Hulu provides a good overview of many of the challenges media owners and content providers face.

Hulu provides TV content and programs for free, online. Its revenues come from pre-roll and side advertising. Its aim is to be the YouTube equivalent for TV programs. It launched in 2008 and quickly became successful, pushing revenues up to $150m and securing content partnerships from the likes of Disney, NBC Universal and News Corp. But in a world where content online has now quickly become available for free from many alternative places and on other different access devices, and without ad interruption or delay, Hulu's owners are already concerned about the long-term viability of their own specialist ad-funded business model. What started out as unique is rapidly becoming common place.

Some of the content provider partners such as Disney want to start charging for their content either by way of subscription or on a pay-as-you-go basis. Others don't want to be tied in only to Hulu and want to make content available in other ways, for example, for the Apple iPad.

As a result, something that had quickly proven to be a success may well tomorrow become a falling star just as quickly, as the online content access environment changes rapidly. Catch-up TV, connected TV devices, the Apple iPad and the emergence of other free online content platforms are undermining Hulu's early market leadership. The Hulu CEO has commented that Hulu is a trail-blazer and that it is prepared to blaze another trail, even if it takes a bit of time.

Hulu has started to respond with Hulu Plus, which is an online paying subscription service giving access on internet-connected TVs and portable devices like the iPad. But this is a major departure from its "free content" theme and starts to compete directly with a new and established set of other subscription-based services. Netflix, for example, had revenues of over $2bn in 2010, is generating high levels of profitability and has become the default provider of video content whether from TV or film. It does charge a subscription so it has established a way of pricing for the industry. But why would a consumer switch to Hulu when Netflix provides a bigger archive of material, is widely advertised and has locked up partnerships with the big guns like Google TV?

Hulu is facing transformational change from all sides, even though the company itself was regarded as a pioneer of the digital revolution at the time of its launch just a short while ago. Catch-up TV players are now easily and widely available for free, online, interactive, net-based TV has been launched and will be ramped up, the iPad and other tablets allow for easy remote download and access of TV and movie content, Google, Apple, Sony and other big guns are muscling into this arena … not a good time for Hulu to start another round of fund-raising!

Meantime behind the scenes, TV broadcasters themselves are in a mild state of panic. The digital landscape is changing so fast that they are struggling to work out their role in this emerging internet TV age. How soon, for example, should the network TV operators release TV shows online without destroying their value in other markets such as DVDs or reruns? How do they maintain the number of monthly cable or satellite subscriptions when more and more people are watching TV content and movies on the internet? Such monthly fees have helped to support TV, especially in the US, for years so watching them decline is alarming. In fact, 2010 saw the first decline in total US cable and satellite subscriptions for decades, with 335,000 fewer households paying for the service. Some of that might be general belt-tightening and cost consciousness after the credit crunch and subsequent slow-down, but many industry watchers such as Sam Schechner of the *Wall Street Journal* believe we are witnessing a sea-change in the way TV broadcasters earn their revenues. In 2010, internet viewing was up 96%, with over three billion videos watched on all formats in the month of December alone. In an interview with the Wall Stree Journal, Hulu's CEO acknowledges that "consumer behavior is changing [and] if you're a content owner you're at risk of being left behind." The difficulty for all parties is deciding on the new business model. In the same article, the head of Time Warner's television arm commented that: "At some point, if enough people turn off cable, then you've got a complete disruption of the business model." This would have a big knock-on impact on all those relying on revenues from it.

The short-term solution has seen TV program makers striking out in all directions to secure wider distribution deals both domestically and overseas. "Leave no stone unturned" is one way of describing their approach. ABC has been building up its own subscription service; NBC is tying up with Comcast; News Corp is looking to take full control of Sky; AOL has acquired Studio Now and 5Minute to give it an extended video platform, it has also acquired Huffington Post to give it a new and unique content and distribution portal online; Amazon has bought LoveFilm and so it goes on. In fact, a new report from PWC predicts a wave of consolidation in the media sector over the next few years as companies search out solutions. They expect TV companies to take advantage of recent temporary increases in TV ad spend (some recovery from the '08/'09 downturn) that have given them a more profitable base and platform, to reach out to step-change their own digital transformations. If they are going to make acquisitions now is probably the last time they'll have the share price strength to do so. Digital is impacting virtually every sub sector of media. It may have started with books and then moved on to music but now it's about all types of products and services. Long-term and sustainable growth is only obtainable from the digital arena.

What other more proactive strategies should media companies adopt? Should they look to the travel industry for a possible guide? Should they adopt a *hybrid* approach providing a mix of traditional and online content and distribution? Many commentators, for example, expect NetFlix.com to be snapped up any day by one of the big established media companies with everyone from Amazon and Microsoft to Disney, Google and News Corp touted as possible bidders. Should they *forward integrate*, for example, to lock up distribution sources? How about abandoning old ways totally and *going completely online*? Alternatives might be to consider other ways of monetizing content and *adding value*, such as providing the definitive library and database about all TVs, films, the actors, writers, directors … everything you need to know. In the meantime *new low cost entrants* will surely continue to emerge, leveraging the "for free" model while attempting to source revenues from ads or by onselling their database. And *niche, specialist operators* will always find a place, for example, by being the hub for all travel or science content and charging accordingly.

If TV broadcasters are expected to face a major challenge, then consider the newspaper industry. That is already right in the middle of one! Just take a look at this recent headline:

"Digital to kill all UK and US newspapers before 2020"

Countries are predicted to experience this extinction according to their shading in Figure 8, those with the lightest shading losing their newspapers first. And of course, whether it is 2020 or 2025 or 2015, whether hard print newspapers and magazines die out completely or there remains a stubborn, small minority who continue to buy, the days of the print-based publishing business as a successful, sustainable and profitable model have gone. With all

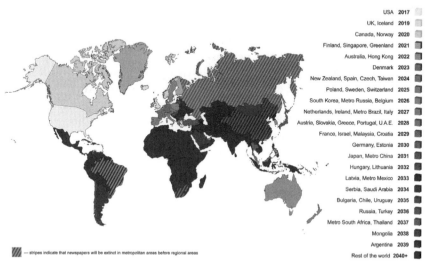

Figure 8 **Newspaper extinction timeline – when newspapers in their current form will become insignificant**
Source: Ross Dawson and Future Exploration Network

papers experiencing continued circulation decline, few in the industry dispute the inevitable trend and most are very actively engaged in working out their new future.

Most of that effort is directed at finding ways to continue to earn revenues while at the same time migrating to the digital world. The most robust and vigorous in pushing down this path has been News Corp. They are experimenting and trialing, confronting the digital change and exploring all the avenues. Most notable has been their 2009 decision to put the *Wall Street Journal* behind a paywall. Despite critics saying it would be the death of the paper, it has in fact been a strong success. In just over a year it had achieved almost 1 million paying online readers generating revenues in excess of $65m a year (according to industry estimates). Most of the WSJ content is behind the paywall with free view to only about one-third of the content and then usually only allowing one click. This "one click free" model is now almost universally copied by those putting content online.

Most importantly for the newspaper industry, a survey by Journalism Online showed that on average the number of monthly visitors to websites that put up paywalls does not completely collapse as had been feared. Provided there was still a reasonable amount of free content people would visit. Most newspapers now using paywalls make archive content freely available and that does sustain interest and visitor levels. The drop-off rate had on average been about 20%. But the survey found that the ad rates that the newspaper or magazine could charge around its paid-for content had barely altered because advertisers found their audience became better targeted, more engaged and likely to spend time on the page and, therefore, better advertising prospects. Also, the ability to engage them with video and other richer forms of advertising in an online environment was found to be valuable.

Encouraged by their success, News Corp next turned its attention to the UK. In 2010 it set the *Times* newspaper online content behind a paywall. While initial reports suggested that the early uptake was slow, the advent of the iPad made the online experience much more enjoyable. Nevertheless, the BBC reported that, at the end of the first six months of the paywall, the *Times* had just about got to 100,000 paying readers, which is in line with early trends for the first six months of the *Wall Street Journal*. But visits to the website have not been maintained. In the first quarter of 2011 they crashed by more than 80% from 21 million visitors per month to just over 2 million.

James Harding, editor of the *Times*, gave his comments on these initial results: "It's very early days but we're hugely encouraged by what we've seen … We'd been engaged in a quite suicidal form of economics – which was giving our journalism away for free. We knew that if we continued to do that we couldn't invest in reporting" – and the paper would soon be out of business!

And therein lies the heart of the matter. Is the best tactic to carry on, give it for free, attract lots of visitors and hope to monetize that traffic with advertising? Or is it better to accept much lower visitor numbers but charge for the content and aim to build a profitable business based on levels of subscription revenue with added targeted advertising? At present there are advocates for both approaches, although the number of "all for free" is rapidly diminishing.

New Media Age recently ran the headline: "Get used to paying for newspaper content". They reflected this gradual shift with more and more papers trialing and experimenting with pay models. Alongside the initiatives at *WSJ* and at News Corp, the *Financial Times* has been another pioneer looking to transform their business into a profitable pay-for-it model. They started out as early as 2002 by experimenting with charging for various pieces of specialist content, in-depth features and other material. They did not make too much of it but over the course of a number of years they have learnt what works for their readers and what does not. Now the *FT* can report success. Content subscription revenue exceeds ad revenue, the number of paying subscribers is about 400,000 and so committed is that user base that the *FT* was able to raise prices 30% in 2010 with almost no reductions in users. Alongside monthly and annual subscriptions there are 24-hour day passes and there remains a significant amount of content still available for free. *FT* CEO Rob Grimshaw thinks that no one can afford to dismiss the idea of developing paid-for content because journalism is valuable. It is significant in that it is reaffirming there is life beyond advertising for online publishing and offers an alternative where it was thought for a long time that no alternative existed.

And now the latest innovation has been the launch by News Corp of The Daily, their specialist "made for iPad and tablet" newspaper. It will be available only in digital form and has been launched with the active support of Apple, with Apple VP of Internet Services side by side with Murdoch at the launch event.

Many in the newspaper industry have welcomed the arrival of the iPad. For the first time it has created a device on which it is fun and easy to read content. Now it's ever more common to ride the train into work and see people with their iPad or other tablet catching up on the news rather than reading it in hard copy print. Murdoch is quoted as saying that The Daily stands at the start of a "digital renaissance": "New times demand new journalism ... The iPad demands that we completely re-imagine our craft."

The Daily is the first digital-only paper and everyone is watching how well it does. But it is transforming. No print production facilities are required, and no costly through-the-night warehouse and truck distribution. Journalists can work and file remotely so there is no need for high-cost office facilities. They can be encouraged to work beyond the 1000-word article and the catchy headline. Now they can drill deeper, mix in video and photos, capture links to other content and make for a much richer experience. Why wouldn't this succeed? As tablet devices inevitably become cheaper, so they will become ubiquitous. Such online devices are already a preferred option for the new generation that is growing up digital and their thirst for news in undiminished. Add in links to socialize the content, to connect it to your Facebook page and it will quickly become popular and widely-used.

The iPad and other tablets have created an "electricity in the newsroom". They are being hailed as the "saving of the newspaper industry". Their arrival has ignited a new sense of hope and passion where previously most were just waiting for the death throes of the paper they were working on. "It's like the early dot com days," said one publisher. If not quite managing to replicate the initiative of The Daily, most papers have rushed out iPad apps and to their surprise their readers have been prepared to pay. It has been the catalyst for pushing up *FT* subscriptions and for encouraging readers to the *Times* on-line. Even hard-core refuseniks like the *Guardian*, still publicly proclaiming the virtues of "free", have launched a pay-for-it iPad app (and subsequently increased its price also by 30%). Conde Nast have launched their iPad app for *Vogue* magazine. *New York*, *The Times*, Dennis Publishing Group ... most everyone now has moved in this direction. Even TV and Radio companies are jumping on the bandwagon with CBS-owned Last.fm launching a mobile app which charges for access to its radio service (otherwise free online) and ITV announcing plans to launch a paywall for its most popular shows.

But it is far too trite and simplistic to assume that the advent of a device, designed by a third party who will want to take their fee too, will be the savior of an industry. Like any competitive market place, this type of digital shake-up will see winners and losers. For example, some publishers have so far done little more than make their content available in digital format. But truly embracing the new medium, taking full advantage of what it can enable, continuously innovating in format and presentation, becoming richer and more topical, updating hourly instead of daily or weekly, establishing partnerships to provide related content, securing wider distribution for example on internet TV as a news or feature app and channel in their own right ... all these things become very possible and very immediately.

Meantime, while embracing the new, most publishers will still need to deal with legacy print and production fixed costs. Old ways of working will need to be worked through and managed accordingly. It's back to the travel industry strategic options: try to succeed as a hybrid both off and online, or go direct online and get out of the old business model? But, for sure, continued change of some kind is surely mandatory. News Corp's chief commercial officer says that they have made their bet on the future and that's to charge for content. Speaking on Radio 4's Today program, the editor of The Times commented that: "It is time to stop giving our journalism away ... We're worried that [the internet's] viral capability wipes us out and actually what's much more important to us is that we create a sustainable economics for the future of journalism online".

Alan Rusbridger, editor of the *Guardian* newspaper, puts a useful historical context to all this:

> With the invention of printing, books by the thousand were tumbling off the presses, and scholars were gripped by a kind of fever as they searched for new ideas about how to organize society. [Quoting the historian, John Man, on the Gutenberg revolution:] "Suddenly, in a historical eye-blink,

scribes were redundant. One year, it took a month or two to produce a single copy of a book; the next, you could have 500 copies in a week. Hardly an aspect of life remained untouched ... Gutenberg's invention made the soil from which sprang modern history, science, popular literature, the emergence of the nation-state, so much of everything by which we define modernity." ... [Many writers are] fascinated by the parallels between that period and today's revolution in communication, which ... is as great as that of Gutenberg. The difference today is that change is happening much faster – so fast that we are, as an industry, collectively suffering from what deepsea divers refer to as the bends. We are travelling through a period of extreme change faster than our corporate bodies can cope with. It's painful – and, if not treated quickly and correctly, can be fatal ... we are living at the end of a great arc of history which began with the invention of moveable type. There have, of course, been other transformative steps in communication during that half millennium ... but what's happening today ... is truly transformative.

Health Care

What impact will digital technology have here? Can we expect the same degree of disruption as we see happening to media and print?

Here's one wonderful example of what we can expect as digital technology puts more power in the hands of the patient.

AliveCor is a start-up US medical company which has developed a simple iPhone app that is being showcased and launched through 2011. It's a case that connects to the iPhone and allows it to function as a clinical-quality electro cardiogram system, keeping track of your heart beat and pulse rate. It is attached directly via a set of electrodes or it can operate wirelessly. It stores and can send data about your heart function anytime, all the time, anywhere, to your doctor, physician, carer or just for your own information.

Source: AliiveCor

Devices like this are going to be part of a growing trend through the course of this decade: the ability to capture data about your body by yourself, to remotely access care and medical advice, to have 24/7 data about your condition available to all in the care system, the ability to get advice without having to travel to 10-minute appointments, the facility to find out your diagnosis now rather than having to wait days on tenterhooks, better monitoring and regulation of your drug regime (what pills are working and what are not, when to increase the dose and when the medication is not needed) ... all in all a more efficient and effective health care system.

That end benefit is critical because the health care system is, of course, facing mounting costs. Not only are more drugs available for more people and we are also living longer, but the global population is projected to continue to rise by a further billion to 7.5 billion by 2020. In addition, the population is aging with c. 10% expected to be aged 65 or more compared with c. 7% in 2010. And somewhat inevitably, older people take more medicine with 80% of those over 75 on some form of medication. Other factors such as the rising number of chronic conditions requiring long-term treatment regimes, increased urbanization squeezing more people into major cities and the consequent impact on health and demand for care, climate change, water shortage, increased poverty all add up to growing pressure on health care systems to provide solutions while at the same time controlling the costs involved.

So, digital technology in health care is less about disruptive change and more about finding ways to deliver better care at lower cost. And a core philosophy for that is giving the patient more control and responsibility to take what care they need only when they need it and in lower-cost ways. Initiatives like AliveCor's app can cut out visits to the doctor, provide immediate reassurance and encourage the patient to stay off the drugs if their body seems to be well or recovering.

Portable medical devices are a big growth market for device manufacturers and Pharma companies. For example, patient-controlled devices to monitor blood pressure, regulate blood sugar levels and cholesterol are all being used today. India is proving a good testing ground for easy-to-use self-care medical devices that are affordable and can be used in the home. It has a large affluent middle class but a relatively poor and overburdened hospital and health care infrastructure, so there is interest and demand for devices that give immediate medical diagnosis, much of which can remove worry or be remedied by a simple visit to the pharmacy. Growth in this area is expected to be supplemented by wide use of mobile video calls, whether via Skype or mobile phone, enabling doctors' and patients to have quick and easy appointments without clogging up doctor and hospital waiting rooms.

Walgreen, the nationwide US pharmacy chain, has been moving to take advantage of digital technologies. Its aim is to be the No.1 preferred destination pharmacy, whether off or online. How is it doing that? It has three particular routes:

1 Using mobile technology platforms to improve delivery of care to patients. Walgreen has established apps on all the main smart phones that feature text alerts and more than 1 million had already signed up by the start of 2011. There is also a function to scan in a barcode of your prescription to automatically trigger a refill, provided it's been pre-approved and signed off by the doctor, to be made up and either sent to your home or to be collected on your next trip to town.

2 An increasing number of kiosks at Walgreen outlets are now the start point for new prescription visits. Patients sign in, setting out brief personal details without filling in pieces of paper and receiving a wait-time. Data inputted into the kiosk creates a medical record which can be accessed by third-party care providers connected to the patient. The records show what drugs are being taken, whether the prescription is being repeated as planned and can provide a full patient history.

Getting all data digital has become a key challenge for those in the health care value chain. There is so much data that keeping up-to-date patient records in hard copy files is just becoming too costly and complex. In addition, the need for immediate up-to-date patient information to be available in real time to a wide range of carers, welfare workers and physicians via remote access is increasing. Walgreen here is looking to play its part in the digitization of the health care industry. Given its market leading position, it can be hoped that other pharmacy chains will follow its lead and the eventual result will be a nationwide digital set of records for all patients, from cradle to grave. It's the kind of transformation that the technology easily enables. The cost savings are significant, the increases in efficiency have a wide-spread effect and keep those who participate in these changes at the leading edge.

3 Walgreen is also trialing initiatives such as an e-Communications program to coordinate care between doctor, pharmacy and patient, an e-Prescribing function to ensure prescriptions are automatically sent by doctor to patients' nearest pharmacy and be ready for collection when they get there, and a MedAdvisor facility to allow online patient consultations and questions from patient to pharmacist.

While there is a sense of the urgency (and sometimes feelings of near panic) in the Media and Print industries, Health care leaders are showing what is possible: "By using new digital technology tools, we can improve the patient experience, get better outcomes and contribute to a more cost effective health care system."

A final example in this industry sector showing how technology can bring change for the good, comes from geneticist and founder of the Pink Army Cooperative, Andrew Hessel. He is pioneering ways to encourage new drug innovation by the big Pharma companies at potentially much lower cost. His focus is on breast cancer and his goal is the elimination of that disease by 2020. To achieve this, he wants to accelerate new drug development and introduction. To encourage Pharma companies, he is advocating new methods that would significantly change the R&D process. He suggests the active use of social media to get people involved in trials. "As biology becomes more digital … open access can make it easier to share ideas, publish protocols and tools, verify results, firewall bad designs, communicate best practices, and more."

Hessel advocates a novel funding idea – directly approaching those who would most benefit from any breakthrough. Why not ask people to invest a small amount in a membership scheme? Finding people willing to participate can be set up on social networking sites and promoted on blogs and medical chat forums. "I don't see open-source drug development having a large effect on the US health economy … But there is room for a few examples to exist, make a real and measurable difference, and inspire others to experiment with nonprofit development. If the Pink Army can treat even a single individual, I will consider the project a tremendous success, although I hope it will grow to treat millions of people with medicines that can only get better and cheaper over time."

Advertising

Saatchi & Saatchi shocked the Ad industry in 2010 with their viral video: *The last advertising agency on earth*. The film talked about the possible death of the traditional ad agency and showed the office of the last one left on earth, which had been preserved as a museum! What was the Saatchi message here? Put simply, it was a wake-up call to the big networks: the world has changed, consumers will choose to watch the content they prefer, not the content ad agencies feel they should watch. Agencies are at risk of being left behind if they do not realize just how fundamental digital and multi-channel has become. Adding a Facebook page to a TV commercial, making that ad available online, setting up a temporary twitter feed during a TV campaign is simply not far-reaching enough and is just scratching the surface.

The Saatchi film was made because many of the traditional ad agencies had for a number of years done very little to truly embrace the digital world. Most had made symbolic hires of "heads of digital". It might have sounded like a good idea but the job became impossible as this person tried almost single-handedly to champion digital communications, educate internal teams, be an advocate in front of clients and try to stop the "let's just make another TV ad" juggernaut. Many well-intentioned and highly-skilled digitally-savvy individuals eventually gave up and left. Their plea for more resources, more skills training, an infusion of more digitally literate people, for commitment and passion stemming right from the CEO to drive a more multi-channel approach and so on all just falling on deaf ears, or perhaps being received with glib assurances of change which never materialized.

With a huge vacuum in the market for digital ideas and talent, some of the established creative agencies lost substantial ground. In their place, the big media networks such as MediaCom have stepped in. They have grabbed a much bigger role for themselves by championing the multi-channel world in media planning and buying. That has let them push up the value chain and try to become centers for excellence in strategy and marketing advisory work, a place for marketing managers and directors to turn for that initial multi-channel advice. But the downside of that route is that, instead of being driven by the insight and ideas of a strong multi-channel creative ideas-led agency, brands now risk being driven straight into a tactical and executional media discussion about where best to place the advertising.

Specialist digital agencies have also emerged to try to seize this new-age high ground. They stand out because of their great passion and enthusiasm and have quickly captured the creative lead for many brands on all things digital. Agencies like AKQA, LBi, Razorfish and RGA have all found themselves as market leaders, sought out by the big global brands wanting innovation and ideas relevant to today's environment and today's consumer. And these agencies have spawned further specialists such as in Mobile or Social Media where there are real experts who know how to put together, for example, the most effective social media buzz around a brand and its customers.

All this development has gone on since around 1999 and the big digital

Plate 1 **Gesture Cube**

Plate 2 **Emotiv EPOC headset**

Plate 3 **Virtual shopping**

Plate 4 **iPhone**

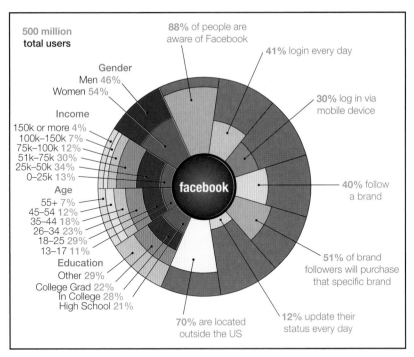

500 million
total users

88% of people are
aware of Facebook

41% login every day

Gender
Men 46%
Women 54%

30% log in via
mobile device

Income
150k or more 4%
100k–150k 7%
75k–100k 12%
51k–75k 30%
25k–50k 34%
0–25k 13%

40% follow
a brand

Age
55+ 7%
45–54 12%
35–44 18%
26–34 23%
18–25 29%
13–17 11%

51% of brand
followers will purchase
that specific brand

Education
Other 29%
College Grad 22%
In College 28%
High School 21%

70% are located
outside the US

12% update their
status every day

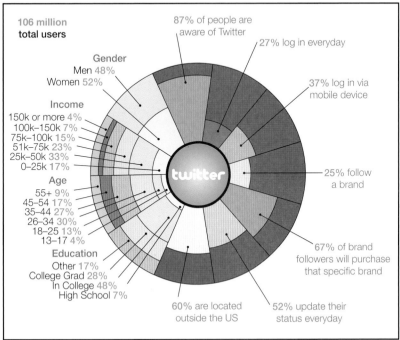

106 million
total users

87% of people are
aware of Twitter

27% log in everyday

Gender
Men 48%
Women 52%

37% log in via
mobile device

Income
150k or more 4%
100k–150k 7%
75k–100k 15%
51k–75k 23%
25k–50k 33%
0–25k 17%

25% follow
a brand

Age
55+ 9%
45–54 17%
35–44 27%
26–34 30%
18–25 13%
13–17 4%

67% of brand
followers will purchase
that specific brand

Education
Other 17%
College Grad 28%
In College 48%
High School 7%

60% are located
outside the US

52% update their
status everyday

Plate 5 **Facebook v. Twitter – a breakdown of 2010 social demographics**
Note: Each segment represents a distinct socio-demographic segment or user behavior type.

Plate 6   **Net TV**

Plate 7   **Restir, Midtown Tokyo**

Plate 8   **Dover Street Market**

Plate 9   **10 Corso Como**

Plate 10

Plate 11

Plate 12　**MyFaveShop**

agencies are now well-established. AKQA employs close to 1000 people worldwide with offices in San Francisco, New York, Washington, London, Berlin, Amsterdam and Shanghai. LBi employs some 2000 people with a score of offices all over the world. And there are other digitally-focused agencies with wide global footprints, all of which have sprung up from nothing in the Web 1.0 days and now compete effectively in the global ad market. And all that is business that the "traditional agencies" have lost. And they lost not just revenue and market share but also, and more pointedly, they lost reputation which they are only now beginning to recover.

Certainly there are some who have responded. Agencies like Wieden + Kennedy and Crispin Porter are two notable exceptions and successes. DDB in Europe is one of the bigger ad networks to make big strides to deliver this multi-channel capability. And WPP is one of the few global networks to manifestly invest in new digital resources and capabilities. These agencies have steadfastly stuck to their philosophy of being "ideas-led" and as communication channel options have proliferated, so they have made it their business to acquire the skills and know-how to provide leading edge solutions in those areas too.

While the big holding agency groups like WPP, Omnicom and Publicis have certainly found the digital wave challenging, they have been responding via a mix of organic growth and acquisitions, often finding local market-independent digital and other agencies to boost share. Publicis has been acquiring agencies such as Razorfish and Chemistry, WPP has taken a more strategic route, for example, launching Possible Worldwide which brings together four regionally successful agencies (Schematic, Bridge, Blue and Quasar) into one global group with the aim of becoming a digital powerhouse for WPP clients and Omnicom has focused on mainstream and global strategic partnerships with the likes of Yahoo, AOL and Microsoft to provide its client brands with unique consumer data and access.

The recovery of the traditional agency groups has been helped by the temporary upturn in TV ad revenues in 2011 following the downturn. The big networks have garnered some breathing space and they now seem determined to use this time to catch up. There may at last be some genuine awakening and recognition of the need for change. Continuing to pay lip service to the challenge is just not appropriate. Bob Jeffrey, CEO at JWT, has recently been making digital change within his own company a priority: "We can no longer just acquire [digital] firms, it's not good enough". Also there's been an announcement from Ogilvy that it plans this year to spend significantly on internal training to increase know-how and awareness. Maybe this time around these ambitious statements of intent and investment will deliver the sea-change required.

Internal training and awareness-building has to be the catalyst if these agencies are going to transform successfully into 2020 winners, and there are now a multitude of highly-praised training programs available. These range from Sweden's Hyper Island which provides a week-long immersive dive into the digital world, to courses and diplomas from the Institute for Direct

Marketing to the proliferation of training agencies who claim to offer skills development in digital.

Omnicom's DDB are an example of one group making these kinds of investments and changes. What they have also done in some locations is merge their "traditional" above-the-line teams with their digital unit, Tribal, and try to develop an integrated in-house client approach which can combine the old ATL skills with the new digital tools and opportunities. It has delivered some good client results but the key here has been co-location. That has been instrumental in establishing internal awareness of multi-channel skills and provided the easy access to them. When the teams are in one building and the channel barriers have been broken down then cooperation and a more integrated approach does become possible. Having the right people together in one building has been found to be key to achieving the desired cross-channel integration and collaboration.

While agencies struggle to find their feet in this world, there are still other approaches being tried and tested. One comes from the consultancy sector. As Tim Hipperson, the former JWT CEO in the UK and now CEO at G2, has put it: "Consultancies are increasingly compensating for left-brain deficiencies in agencies. Marketers have introduced new advisors into their cabinet to fill skill gaps at traditional agencies." Their key value-add and insight is to provide the analytical and strategic insight that helps brands navigate their way through this complex multi-channel world. They can't and wouldn't want to get involved in the creative process. But the likes of Accenture have developed "Interactive teams" staffed by, for example, ex-Procter & Gamble brand managers who can combine their real world understanding of developing the next-year marketing strategy and budget plan with the rigorous insight of Accenture data number crunchers. They can develop complex models looking at which channels have delivered more ROI for the brand and which combination would potentially add the most value. In effect, they write the business case that says how much to spend, where, when and how and prepare the platform that means the creative and comms brief to the agency can be clear, prioritized and direct.

In Tim Hipperson's view, there is no need for agencies to cede this strategic ground to the likes of Accenture and other "new cabinet advisors". Rather, this creates a big opportunity for agencies to establish their *own* consultancy/advisory teams. This could become a natural evolution for their existing strategy and planning capabilities which in some agencies already provide a consulting-like service. If agencies can find the right people with experience to engage the CMO in the multi-channel debate then that could be a great route back for them to recapture their original role as the marketing chief's key strategic partner.

As we all eventually discover there is no Holy Grail solution. It will always be challenging for one agency to be a one-stop shop that can provide all the answers. It is however clearly essential to get as close as possible to some kind of skill and expertise platform that can make the best possible decisions for brands and clients.

One advocate with a contrary perspective is Tim Williams. He argues that trying to find an effective full service multi-channel agency is futile. In his book, *Positioning for Professionals*, he argues pointedly to "forget full service". His view is that it's just not possible to find such a company and far better to select a group of specialists and get them to collaborate. He argues that marketers are in search of specific solutions to specific problems in specific industry sectors, not looking for generalists with experience across diverse categories. "No client ever buys a 'wide range of expertise,' but rather a specific kind of expertise."

And reflecting this sort of thinking, it's instructive to see how an organization like Unilever approaches this challenge. They are a highly sophisticated and experienced organization with leading-edge brand development and marketing skills. Their idea is to have specialist agencies for specialist purposes but to bring them together in regular forums to share ideas, methods, best practices and approaches. They want the best of breed in each area but recognize that they, as the brand owners, need to take responsibility for collaboration, cooperation and finding the best solution. That is usually done each quarter in day-long sessions and agencies are scored on their willingness to collaborate and share. Often times the agencies will be focused on planning the next quarter campaign and they have to be willing to go with and support whoever comes up with the best idea. Around the table might be the ATL TV agency, the digital team, the direct marketing group, PR, social media and whatever other agencies seem most relevant.

If the PR company comes up with the best idea and approach in the judgment of the Unilever marketers (and, right or wrong, they are the ones who are paying), then all the agencies are expected to come up with plans to support that. Sure, there's still a bit of a turf war and fight over budgets but the marketing group are taught to manage that efficiently and at the end of the day the long-term potential value of the relationship means agencies will usually toe the line.

This approach works for Unilever which has been developing it for many years and has evolved the ways and means to manage and control the process. It represents a very pragmatic solution to the multi-channel challenge and allows for all the necessary expertise to come together. It relies on intelligent management from the marketers who have to use their judgment on what will be most appropriate, and be sure not to leave any obvious marketing routes unexploited.

Digital has created this rush of new challenges and most agencies and marketers have had little time to build up real case-study expertise on what is the right solution. As David Ogilvy said many years ago: "Half the money I spend on advertising is wasted, and the trouble is I don't know which half". In today's fast-paced world it's even more difficult to get it right and so it requires ever more careful planning and management to maximize the chances of success.

* * * * *

All the industry sectors discussed here – Travel, Media and Newspapers, Health Care, Advertising – are facing issues and challenges which are no different from every other sector in the economy. Banking, Manufacturing and Automotive, although not facing digital meltdown yet, are all having to stare digital technology in the face and work out their response. As mentioned, those that directly face the consumer are very much more in the vanguard, being the pioneers who have to work out solutions without reference to established best practices and lessons learnt. They have to work it out for themselves, make their own mistakes, create their own roadmaps and forge future development paths.

We can look back to the wave of reengineering that swept the business world during the 1990s. What took place at that time provides some analogy to today's revolution. What fuelled that restructuring was not technology but the increasing competitive threats of globalization and the low-cost competitors that suddenly found access to new countries and markets. Companies which had long enjoyed local market dominance and easily maintainable price premiums suddenly found that that was no longer sustainable. Manufacturing industry, especially, came under intense pressure then from Asian competition who brought with them new working practices, new agile ways of assembly, lower-cost sourcing, product innovation, new marketing techniques, aggressive pricing and so on. The only way for companies to survive was to look at a radical restructure of how they did business so that they could compete. It brought about a fundamental root-and-branch review of cost and process and was given the label "reengineering". So popular was it that one of the leading consultancies promoting this type of reform at the time, CSC Index, had a waiting list for its seminars. Within one 12-month period, 235 of the Fortune 500 top corporations had attended its 2-day seminars at Pebble Beach. Many of those attendees were the company CEOs.

What were they coming to hear? The message was "adapt or die". The need for fundamental change was apparent. New companies were emerging without the legacy systems, costs and processes that were stifling innovation in the established companies. They were fleet of foot, utilized global sourcing partnerships, were speedier to market, were constantly adapting and improving and reducing costs. And, although the threat may have been most evident in manufacturing, it was growing in every sector.

"Reengineering" became the buzz word of the 1990s. As we move towards 2020, the current buzz is "digital transformation" but, whatever we call it, it requires the same thinking, approach, commitment and readiness to change. The stark lessons from the reengineering days are easily captured:

1 Digital transformation requires CEO and C-Level commitment and recognition to put this top of the agenda.
2 No stone can be left unturned; there can be no "sacred cows"!

3 The whole workforce needs to be engaged, to understand the need for change, the urgency of doing that and their role and contribution to it.

4 It takes time. Fundamental transformation does not happen overnight. It requires a full 3-year roadmap of step-by-step review and renewal.

5 There needs to be a clear vision and strategy that explains why we are doing this and, most critically, defines the end-game: What will be the benefits for this company and its customers? Describing that as "survival" is not enough. It ideally needs to be a quantifiable set of benefits that everyone can understand and identify.

While these lessons are simple and maybe even obvious, how many companies really approach change by wholeheartedly embracing these ideas? Many will move forward with some incremental plan, some tinkering around the edges, some tick-box activity or investment which gives a headline to shareholders but doesn't really take the big opportunity on board. Others might try to buy their way out of trouble, acquiring digitally savvy competitors at too-high prices. (A case in point is Time Warner's disastrous merger with AOL which led to a $99bn loss! and a very poor result for TW shareholders who swapped TW for AOL stock.)

M&A (Mergers and Acquisitions) can of course be a necessary and effective way to restructure a portfolio of businesses and assets but the real opportunity remains the transformation of the way the company reaches out to its customers, becomes more innovative and creative, provides a new and more engaging experience, sees multi-channel as a chance to win more market share (and not as some bewildering and impossible complexity), examines what digital technology can do to provide more insightful data and information, to react more quickly, to cut out stifling systems and silos, establish a renewed sense of purpose and conviction and to take the company forward as a future market leader.

11 Impact on Retail and Property Sectors

Retail Week, the UK trade magazine, shocked its audience at the start of 2011 with the headline: "How many stores does a retailer need?" They went on to say: "The growing opportunity of online retail combined with the heavy costs of operating stores would prompt some to answer 'not very many'." This comes from a trade body that is highly influential and which has historically focused much of its news and features on the value and benefits of in-store development and new store design.

The *Financial Times* also ran a feature on the topic: "Landlords fear web shopping fashion." The *FT* went on to comment that "internet shopping threatens to turn stores into glorified product showrooms where consumers view goods before ordering them more cheaply and conveniently online … 'The internet is definitely a disruptive technology, and property developers are very nervous about its growth,' says Andrew O'Donnell, commercial director of John Lewis." "The property world has been in denial," says Richard Hyman of Verdict. By his calculations, "the growth of online shopping has added the equivalent of 25m sq ft of virtual retail capacity … almost every retailer you think of has got too many shops … This sentiment is bound to grow as more and more revenue comes through their websites."

The shock of the online age is far-reaching and transforming. The old ways of managing and building a retail business no longer apply. Just adding space could prove to be a financial disaster as this decade unfolds. The multi-channel environment is beginning to dominate and retailers especially are on the front line facing these changes.

While many retailers have made great strides in building up their on-line capability, they nearly all have assumed that they can at the same time continue to grow by also adding more floor space. It's got to a point where, despite the growth of online and the obvious shift to a multi-channel environment, most retailers have just carried on allowing their vast property and stores team to continue to build:

▷ Retailers are committed to step up store expansion plans in 2011. In research by real estate brokers Richard Ellis, over 50% of the 212 retailers interviewed said they plan to open 10 or more stores during the next 2 years, with 28% looking at more than 30 stores and 19% saying they planned to open more than 40 new stores. Indeed some like Forever 21, Aldo and Superdry have plans for more than 100.
▷ Sainsbury's have announced plans to open 2.5 million square feet of space in just the next 12 months.

> We are pleased to be opening more space proportionally to the business than any other grocer.

And in the same press release:

> Referring to our online customers, we find that when customers shop online they become more loyal and we are very happy with the profitability of our online operation.

Is all that consistent? Is there a coherent strategy here?

▷ New retailers continue to come to market looking for aggressive expansion of retail space. New concept retailers like SuperGroup, DNA Lingerie and Clas Ohlson are competing for new sites, alongside the established chains and even the value retailers like Poundland (*Retail Week*).
▷ Research by Evolution shows that UK grocery retailers alone plan to open some 25 million square feet of new space by 2015. And the big 4 grocers will dominate that expansion accounting for some 70% plus of that new space. In the meantime specialist retailers will continue to grow by adding "virtual capacity" through their internet operations.
▷ US Retailers plan to open 65,000 new stores over the next two years according to research by Retail Lease Trac and RBC including chains like Wal-Mart and Target. However there still remains a large amount of empty space on the market.

So what's happening out there? It seems that even the most sophisticated retailers, from Tesco to Wal-Mart, are continuing with relatively aggressive programs for opening new store space. At the same time, the ability to achieve a successful return on investment from the physical stores portfolio is becoming harder to achieve. And they continue with this old traditional strategy of driving growth through more space even though – and despite the very evident signs – the traditional way of doing things is beginning to run out of steam and may just no longer be appropriate.

There are four key pieces of evidence to show that the days of driving retail growth by adding more space are numbered:

1 In the UK during the 1990s space expansion domestically could be justified among the major grocers as their market share was at a relatively lower level of some 45%. Now they account for 75%. Retail analyst Jonathan Pritchard from Oriel believes there is just a limited amount of real growth left available for them as they have the market saturated.

2 Analyst David McCarthy of Evolution has run the numbers and estimates that, to get a double digit return on this level of space expansion, the 18 million square feet of extra space that the grocers are committing to would have to add some £20 billion of incremental sales. And in his view this level of extra space-driven sales growth is "unlikely [because] when high sales density space comes on stream faster than demand is growing, there will be, at minimum, indigestion with weak like-for-like sales and disappointing new store performance."

3 With little real growth in the economy, online is taking market share. IMRG estimate that 17% of all retail sales in the UK are now purchased online. This strong percentage share of market is increasing, particularly in consumer electronics, computer hardware, software and accessories and apparel and footwear. These sectors are growing at "double digits" online while the offline channels are at best flat. In the US, Forrester Research have shown that 67% of all consumers "do some shopping online" and that online sales are forecast to have annual growth rates of around 8%. Again this is against a backcloth of limited to no growth in store-based sales.

   Clive Black of Shore Capital believes there just is not the same need and justification for so much store space in the next 5 years and beyond. He thinks that retailers will have to start thinking much more flexibly about shopper options, home delivery and the ease and complementary nature of online shopping.

4 Retail profit margins are already thin and these multi-channel changes are putting increasing pressure on profitability and on the viability of retail space. It's time to significantly question a retail bricks 'n mortar-dominant strategy.

To illustrate this, let's take a look at what it takes to break even on retail space and make a return on that substantial capital investment.

The bottom line is that, for most retailers, it will only require a reduction in store sales of c.15% for those stores to be plunged below break-even and into a loss-making situation. Retail margins are generally just too thin to sustain substantial shifts in the way consumers buy.

Table 1 shows just how dramatic the impact of the ever-growing shift to online can be. Numerous traditional retail groups have already disappeared from the mall and from the high street. Others are struggling and their ability to survive has been made more acute by the credit crunch and its impact

Table 1 Impact on store profitability of 15% consumers buying online instead of in-store

	Current	15% reduction
Store sales	100	85
Percentage cost of goods	75%	76.5%*
Net cost of goods	75	65
Gross margin	25	20
Fixed costs	20	20
Net operating margin	5	0

*reduced supplier discounts on lower sales volume

on jobs, confidence and spending patterns. How many more retail groups are going to be in the next wave of casualties?

It all comes down to retailers needing to acknowledge the impact of the multi-channel world and, rather than resist it, go along with it: make it the friend rather than enemy and explore just how to take advantage of it.

The key insight is to accept that retail space must now have a different role to play. It is gradually ceasing to be a bricks 'n mortar-led world and it needs a new strategic approach that identifies *what bricks where and in what size and in what format and with what purpose.*

One of the largest real estate property developers, Land Securities (the c.$10bn quoted UK plc), is among the few who are explicitly acknowledging this changing retail landscape. While they remain bullish overall about the prospects for continued retail property investment (and as property developers it's hard to see them taking any other view), nevertheless they accept that there are structural changes on the way. For them it's about seeing the eventual demise of secondary retail estate and the gradual concentration into fewer but bigger centers.

> While online shopping may increase competition for some retailers, we also believe the growth of multi-channel retailing, digital marketing and mobile technology will create new opportunities for retailers with access to high quality retail space. Over time the potential casualties of the structural changes are likely to be shops in medium sized towns where there is a low quality offer and poor facilities, especially those located close to larger, competing centres. Rental recovery is likely to reflect these trends, becoming polarised across UK towns and cities according to the level of vacancies and the attraction of individual assets. We also anticipate the polarisation to be reflected in the investment market, where the number and range of potential buyers favour prime assets.

> The consumer preference for the choice provided by big centres will mean that retail sales will keep moving to the biggest locations [into 2011 and beyond].

As the retail world wakes up to these challenges, there are probably five different strategies available:

1   Despite the evidence, a determinedly **bricks-led approach** could still work. But it will have to be based on a fundamental understanding of customer need and a view that the retail space can be made so exciting and unique and attractive that, "Well, why wouldn't customers want to come and visit?"

This in effect makes the space a destination, a place to come to. But this is a very hard thing to achieve. Today there are only a small group of high-end brands that could genuinely be said to offer that type of retail experience. We can think of Apple, Nike, maybe Abercrombie & Fitch, luxury retailers such as Gucci, Louis Vuitton, Prada and perhaps a few others, but how many would you get into your car to drive to or take the bus to on a busy day in cold wet weather?

To make this work the stores have got to be amazing. Here are some examples taken from a recent poll of the top 10 global destination boutiques as experienced and described by the innovative and creative team at Handbag.com.

▷ *Restir, Midtown Tokyo* (Plate 7)
   "Hiroaki Takashita threw down the gauntlet to his rivals within the $167 billion luxury goods industry when he founded his first Restir boutique in Kobe, Japan in 2000. When it came to his third store in newly developing midtown Tokyo, coming up with the same old same old wasn't an option. Where to start with the 'wow' factor here? Futuristic 30-ft walls of LED plasma displaying adverts for art installations in the 1st floor gallery, black marble floors, black and burgundy interiors designed by French architect Laur Meyrieux, concierge desk, and mega brand pieces from Marc Jacobs, Balenciaga, McQueen, Yves Saint Laurent and a range of Chanel bags that are unique to this store. NB. This is only the second boutique outside Chanel's own stores Karl Lagerfeld has bestowed this honour upon."
▷ *Dover Street Market, London* (Plate 8)
   "Bare walls, steel beams and six floors of purist high fashion displayed in a wacky way in collaboration with the designers themselves, such as Raf Simons, Alber Elbaz and Junya Watanabe. What else might you expect from the intellectual Japanese design guru, Rei Kawakubo, who was behind the concept and direction of this über modern retail space? The Comme des Garcons designer could have put this anywhere but New York lost out to lucky old London. (And hip Hoxton to stuffy Mayfair?). Spacious, stark, pretentious and arty, come here to ogle weird but wonderful designer clothes and art-meets-fashion installations, sniff the latest Comme fragrance, buy a limited edition fashion piece or simply people-watch."
▷ 10 *Corso Como, Milan* (Plate 9)
   "This 13,000 sq ft shop combines art space, bookstore, antique homewear section, groovy restaurant as well as crucial fashion items of the season.

Founder, Carla Sozzani was inspired by oriental bazaars and 1970s London boutique, Biba for her shop. Carla's look-alike sister, Franca, is editor-in-chief of Vogue Italia which is why a lot of trends you see in the revered mag you can also find at 10 Corso Como. Crucially chic with whitewashed walls and a rustic central courtyard cut off from the crazy Milanese traffic, this becomes a haven of tranquillity during Milan fashion week. A ploy to lure fashionistas away from rival boutiques on Via Montenapoleone perhaps?"

2 An alternative that is growing in interest as a way forward is the **Showcase strategy**. In this approach, the store becomes the showcase for the product. But crucially, store profitability no longer exists as a metric in its own right. It's now more about total channel profitability. Instead of building silos, the whole set of customer channel interactions needs to be captured and effectiveness measured in a genuinely integrated and multi-channel way.

So in the UK, using *Retail Week* research, a showcase property strategy probably requires a maximum of 30 stores (150 in the US?). These would be sited in the major malls and conurbations. "That size of property portfolio combined with a strong online strategy is likely to be a typical multi-channel strategy in the years ahead ... tomorrow's multiple retailers won't need to be in second-tier towns. Far better to do multi-channel well and have a smaller number of stores that provide the retail experience. Many sizable towns and cities will fall into this 'second-tier bracket'. Some property sites may never see retail again. It's not a pretty outlook but it is inevitable. The march of multi-channel will reinforce the divide between winners and losers".

The Dixons Stores Group is one retailer which is trying to move in this direction. Focused on the electricals sector, this corporation has been in the firing line for the past 10 years as online has continued to erode store sales. And while the company has fought back with its own strong online propositions, it has nevertheless had to contend with a large legacy real estate suffering slowly declining sales and profitability. Rather than abandon real estate completely, Dixons is slowly evolving to a "showcase store" strategy where it will have a predominance of large out-of-town category stores, presence in major malls and also on a few primary high street locations.

Dixons has been revamping its entire store portfolio over the past 3 years under the leadership of CEO John Browett. It now has 25 megastores or showcase stores placed strategically around the UK. It has also redesigned its other stores, closing around 10% and targeting each one with aggressive like-for-like sales increases if they are to survive. In addition a new format called Dixons "Black" has been introduced, aimed at providing that compelling/exciting destination store experience.

Dixons today unveiled a new fascia, Black, which takes a radically different approach to electrical retailing. The 15,000 sq ft store in Birmingham is positioned as "the ultimate place to get up close with the most wanted gadgets around". The retailer has created a highly differentiated electricals retail format designed to attract shoppers who want the latest technology and designer brands in an inspirational store environment. There are no large walls of stock in boxes. What you see are play areas allowing you to interact with latest merchandise, sofas and comfortable chairs, children's gadget area, sound and vision studio, a "must-have" Objects of Desire centre and a Tech Guys Know-How station. It's all done in black, no exterior daylight and intended to absorb the customer into an engaging space and experience.

This is a make-or-break investment for Dixons. Get it wrong and they will will face serious financial problems. Get it right and they are building and establishing the new platform that can take them forward for the next five years or more. Early signs from Dixons "Black" have been encouraging and there are now reasonable prospects for the corporation as a whole, even though the margins in its others stores continue to struggle. Broker forecasts reflect this transformation: "Consumers rate the new formats as superior to competition, they do provide a step-change showcase experience and if Dixons can continue to restructure their portfolio, things are set to significantly improve."

3   An alternative strategy is to make the store the focal point. **Build the multi-channel capability around the store** itself.

My old stamping ground, Argos, set themselves up that way and seized real competitive advantage with their integrated multi-channel business model that revolves around the store. That MCE approach now drives 43% of all Argos sales. It manifests itself principally through two major initiatives, both established in the early Web 1.0 days. These are "Ring 'n Reserve" and "Click 'n Collect". Both drive the consumer into the store, both seek to minimize home-delivery costs, both initiatives steer the final transaction at the store level where the opportunity for further impulse or considered purchasing is available and of course encouraged. Click 'n Reserve online accounted by itself for 22% of all final sales in 2010. In addition, Argos has available in-store its extensive catalog. That's another reason to visit the store but it also combines the leisure and convenience of home/family selection with final in-store purchasing. In-store and online, Argos makes available its entire product range so that consumers can select via catalog or kiosk. And that works too. More than 40% of home delivery sales come from orders placed in-store with plans to provide more kiosks and make the user selection more user-friendly. It's anticipated that in-store kiosk ordering will continue to grow.

So here we have as developed and integrated an MCE model as can be found anywhere in the world. And it's all built around leveraging the real estate assets and aggressively combining stores and online into one integrated experience. To the credit of Argos they now have 10 years' experience of learning how to make this work, how to improve upon it and how to make the multi-channel interactions combine as seamlessly as possible. And not surprisingly they are learning how to integrate mobile into this store-based philosophy and approach. *Internet Retailing* sees Argos as a leader in integrated store-based retailing providing compelling reasons to visit the store and keep that experience alive.

4   Use **kiosks** to maximize total sales. Recent research by Internet Retailing also looked at how retailers addressed the problem of being out of stock in the store. Most consumers just walk out and either visit a rival store or wait till they're back home and search for the product online. However in the research, 81% of consumers said that, given the option, they would be likely or very likely to order an out-of-stock item using an online kiosk while they were still in the store, if that facility were made available to them.

In the experience of GSI Commerce's Steve Davis, if you find yourself out of stock and leave your consumer to walk out of the door, then you've probably lost that sale. However, in this multi-channel world there's a fantastic opportunity to "extend the shelf space". If you have space to offer 5 items in the store then you should be able to offer a further 20 product options from the same category or range, but do so online. Stores should enable consumers to search online, and easily rather than having to wait in-line or find a helpful member of staff who will do it for you.

But how many stores do that today? How many times do we browse in-store and walk out without at any point checking to see what else might be available from the rest of the product range not featured on the shelf? If there is a kiosk, there's usually just one, it's often not working and/or is tucked away in a dark unfriendly corner at the back of the shop. It needn't be that way! The cost of retail estate is so high that it is vital to maximize every consumer interaction. Every time someone walks out without purchasing, that is lost income and stores should be able nowadays to take advantage of digital technology to optimize that consumer's experience. How many people walk out of Tesco or Wal-Mart without buying anything? That is a very small percentage and retailers in other sectors need to find their own ways of taking advantage of technology to capture that consumer interest and convert it into a sale.

Latest research from IRCE, however, shows that on average retailers have only been spending around 2.5% of their revenues on technology. But dedicated online merchants spend closer to 10%-plus and it's not so surprising to see why Amazon remains such a dominant online player when you discover it spends closer to 20% of its revenue on continued site and technology enhancement. So are there any retailers that are prepared to make the kind of investment required to capture this "total sales" opportunity?

At House of Fraser, the UK fashion retailer, they are trying to tackle precisely this problem head-on. They have invested a lot in store-staff education to make them feel that they are part of and need to contribute to a multi-channel orientation and structure. So, store managers and till staff are incentivized. "If the shop is out of stock, then we can still aim to close the sale there and then but complete it online. To win the hearts and minds of store staff we pay commission on what we call assisted sales. We want store staff to see multi-channel not as a threat but as an opportunity."

John Lewis, the UK department store, is also looking to develop the same sort of approach and make those of its staff who interact with customers feel a sense of responsibility to ensure the sale is completed, through whatever channel is appropriate. And there's planned to be especial focus here on big ticket items which are often arranged for next-day or later home delivery so an online solution is just as appropriate.

Matalan are looking to capitalize on this area of opportunity. They are considering a combination of staff education and provision for them and the customer of the facility to shop in-store online: "We recognise a shift in our customers' shopping behavior, and are looking to use technology to service customer requirements, however they wish to engage with us." So Matalan are rolling out touch screen kiosks, enabling in-store customers to also browse the retail site online and access the entire product range. In the US, Kohl's, Macy's and Nordstrom among others are also in the process of trialing and rolling out more in-store kiosks and looking at similar ways to optimize the store as a focal point for their multi-channel ambitions.

Adidas, too, are getting into in-store kiosks in their stores They wanted to enrich the in-store experience, encourage people to spend longer in the store and use that time to make them aware of new products and new ranges. To achieve this they built central video consoles showing top football tricks and skills from leading Adidas-sponsored football players like Messi, Kaka and David Villa. You could watch the videos but you can also download them onto your mobile phone so you can show them to friends and watch them later. The download comes via a simple Bluetooth link and makes full use of proximity marketing techniques. The download also came with links to a short form configured for mobile website where users can sign up for more info and, if so motivated, purchase the pair of the soccer shoes being featured. There is also the opportunity to go online and download a free Adidas mobile app, but it was felt that the Bluetooth link should be the priority because it was immediate, quick and easy and required no action. The Bluetooth link automatically picks up the content.

This initiative has been adopted by Adidas around the world and research has shown that it has encouraged more time and engagement with their Brand plus additional purchasing.

5 Segment the customer base by channel. Retailers have typically looked at their markets in a singular way. They develop their product proposition and format and roll that out across the country they're operating in. There may be some local variation in stock and price but broadly it's the same approach. It's only if a retailer goes overseas into a new geography that that product/format/price proposition gets reviewed, and then not very fundamentally. After all, the thinking goes, "This is our brand, it's what we are and therefore if we're in a new place we have to make that work." However, once again, the multi-channel world is starting to show some leading exceptions:

▷ Prada is targeting its growth in sales in the US and looking to use online to especially reach the "remote shopper segment", shoppers who are too far away to reach a store. It is looking for c.40% of its total US sales to come from online by 2015 and expects 50% of that to come from this segment. The consequence is that it is on a journey to make the online experience as "close to the in-store experience" as possible.

▷ Kohl Group, the US department store, uses its website to specifically target the segment of women shoppers aged 25 to 34 and increased its sales by c.50% in 2010. It is now the 43rd largest online retailer.

▷ Whitney Automotive, the US auto parts distributor, has focused its business to target the online sales growth. It is especially after the small business customer and has transformed itself from a catalog-only distributor to one with more than 80% of its sales online. When that gets to 90% it expects to stop distributing its catalog.

▷ Express Inc., the apparel retailer, has decided to focus on online for its sales growth rather than open more stores. Its online marketing specifically focuses on the 18- to 30-year-old who it has found to be the most responsive to online activity. This now supplements its 500-strong US store portfolio.

▷ Arcadia, the UK fashion group who have become reluctant converts to multi-channel, have finally acknowledged this trend and recognized what its young customer profile is looking for: They do not expect to add as much store space as they have in the past. They are planning to consolidate their store base, cut the total number of outlets and put more investment into their online operations.

*　*　*　*　*

Whatever strategy retailers adopt, it is clear that standing still is not an option. The multi-channel world is going to continue to evolve, and fast!

▷ Research by Forrester shows that 65% of all western European adults with access to the internet start researching a considered product online. 64% of that group say they are "substantially influenced" by their online research, choosing what to buy and whether to buy online or go to a store.

▷ Similar research from Forrester shows that 49% of shoppers who shopped in this way had selected a particular retailer through their online research but ended up purchasing the product from a different retailer. The main reason was that when they visited the store they found the product they wanted was out of stock.

▷ Multi-channel shopping is expected to account for 38% of all US retail sales by 2012, which would represent $1.1 trillion dollars of retail spend influenced or made in this way (Deloitte).

▷ Multi-channel-influenced sales are the "fastest growing category" of sales, expecting high growth over the three years of 2011 through 2013 (Forrester).

▷ While the influence of multi-channel varies by sector and by age group, the biggest spenders online are the higher socio-economic groups (Deloitte).

▷ According to Deloitte research on the multi-channel transformation, software, hardware, electronics, books, music, movies, appliance and tools, pet supplies, auto parts and apparel have all shown themselves to be particularly susceptible to multi-channel retailing. That wide range is expected to expand to cover all categories with equal force and emphasis.

Case Study: Outlet Stores

A report by Euro Retailing at the beginning of 2011, talked about retail demand for new space for designer outlet/secondary market malls. In a detailed survey it found the attractiveness of physical retail investment was coming seriously under threat. The key dynamic is that designer brands are beginning to see online as the dominant distribution channel and are slowly reappraising the value of their store base and the number of physical stores they need.

Brands see eBay especially as leading the online assault on the value of their real estate offerings. Already 59% of items put up for sale are new, not seconds and this proportion is expected to continue to rise. And eBay has even now set up its own dedicated outlet store at outlet.ebay.com which directly cuts out the bricks 'n mortar designer outlet store and attracts most all the designer brands.

Patrick Munson, who is Head of Sales at eBay, has commented that eBay expects its online outlet sales to grow strongly and that its current 5% market share is targeted to triple to 15%. He also claimed that they have taken away 14% of what had previously been bricks 'n mortar sales. Munson believes this must be the most efficient solution for brands – no staff, no infrastructure costs, no capital outlay and no long term commitments. There may be a short-term exploratory variable cost, but it it is still relatively easy for a brand to open up the multi-channel opportunity.

Other outlet centers are meantime responding to eBay's "wake-up call" by reviewing how they can make the physical outlet centre shopping experience more compelling and enjoyable. "We need to research more about what our shoppers are looking for and the extent to which people prefer online to offline. We can no longer be complacent about online competition and what it means for our future store portfolio."

12 Organizational and Structural Solutions

If there were any doubt about the strategic necessity and value of pursuing a multi-channel approach, then here are two pieces of compelling evidence:

▷ McKinsey research shows that:

  – Multi-channel customers can be up to 25% more profitable than single-channel customers.
  – An effective multi-channel approach can lead to savings of up to 15%.

▷ Deloitte research shows that:

  – Companies with strong multi-channel capabilities are expected on average to enjoy cumulative sales growth at a rate 30% faster than single-channel companies.

Source: Imtiaz Kaderbhoy

  – Multi-channel customers spend 82% more per transaction than single-channel customers.
  – While it varies by product group and sector, on average 17% of all transactions in the 2010 survey can be defined as multi-channel, showing a clear mix and combination of channel interactions. That percentage is growing all the time as multi-channel access and technology continues to develop.

For companies that have decided they are ready to start the transformation process, then a necessary early step is working up the business case. How long will it take? What investment in people, time and capital will be required? What are the risks? Is the proposed pace of change fast enough or too fast? How do we manage the changes with our customers and with our staff? What will be the ROI?

How do companies go about establishing that business case? Here are three case studies showing how the Royal Shakespeare Company, ING Bank and GUS plc went about things, and a brief McKinsey insight piece.

Royal Shakespeare Company (RSC)

The RSC is a global brand name. It stages highly acclaimed Shakespeare and other plays and productions at its home theatre in Stratford as well as other venues such as the National Theatre in London. But as "famous" as its brand was, the RSC was not selling enough tickets and needed to find new sources of revenue growth. The challenge had become multi-channel because potential customers were looking online, contacting box offices direct by phone, visiting theatres in person, dealing with ticket agencies in different countries and buying through friends and patrons. The RSC had no up-to-date database or collected view of its customers: who they were, where they came from, who might be loyal high spenders and, assuming they existed, what channels they came through. They realized there was plenty of opportunity to improve by getting better insight and understanding of their multi-channel customer. It was only going to be with this insight that they would be able to start to take advantage of this multi-channel world and to market to and interact with their customers in the channels most convenient to *them*.

The RSC had so much data and information that they decided that they would capitalize upon it. They took a big step and hired Accenture. The goal was to crunch through seven years' worth of ticket-buying data. They wanted to establish a new and true RSC audience database that provided segmentation by channel, by demographic, by country and by number of transactions. Going forward, the database would be automatically updated by every new customer interaction, no matter what the channel of communication.

The results have more than justified the time and investment. The audience database of active customers has grown by 30% and the number of ticket buyers has increased by more than 50% to 320,000. The number of "regulars" or repeat purchases has increased by 70% to nearly 70,000. What's more, the marketing activity can now be better targeted. (At its most simplistic, online buyers can be sent an email instead of a physical mailing and, at least, online can be recognized as the primary means of communication for certain key consumer segments.) This saves time and money and has a much better response rate than the previous mass-mailing activity. Revenue growth targets have now been met and the executive team of the RSC are delighted with the initiative: "The ... model enables us to have much more sophisticated relationships with our audiences." "For example, insights gleaned from the audience analyses spurred the RSC to launch a promotion targeting 16- to 25-year olds [with a £5 ticket deal] ... This campaign, alone, has attracted 33,000 new young theatregoers. The RSC is now well positioned to continue building audience loyalty and market share in the future."

ING Bank

Dutch bank ING now has a powerful database and multi-channel customer intelligence. But it needed a wake-up call to change and develop that. The catalyst was increasing evidence that the Bank's marketing campaigns were losing effectiveness. From research, they found that much of their marketing was just not perceived as relevant by the Bank's customers. Campaign effectiveness and profitability had dropped by as much as 65%. The Bank's organizational structure, processes, applications, and heavy reliance on direct mail were not meeting the needs of a multi-channel bank with a strong internet focus. Each channel to market had its own database, its own team, its own strategy and targets. They might all be part of the same banking organization but they were in effect mini business silos doing their own thing.

The lack of a centralized coordinated cross-channel approach meant that the entire process of running an outbound marketing campaign – from the initial briefing to the final execution – took between 16 and 22 weeks. To compound the problem, it took 6 to 8 weeks for marketers to have a clear picture of the performance of a campaign. For some products like mortgages, this entire process could take as long as 6 months.

ING went through a 15-month project that involved a budget of more than €5 million and around 50 full-time employees from marketing, IT, customer intelligence, and the different channels to build a new multi-channel marketing program that would overcome the old problems. For instance, the separate data warehouses had to be integrated and then modified in order to support real-time centralized multi-channel campaigns. They not only had to be able to provide up-to-date information to managers in head office who needed to make decisions in real time but they also had to be accessible and user-friendly to support new desktop applications in all 300 branches and the Bank's call centers.

ING made some fundamental changes to its organizational structure to enable centralized and automated campaign management. In the past, the different channels would decide which campaigns they would run. Instead, a centralized customer intelligence team was established to plan and execute all campaigns. Importantly, this meant a power shift from the channels to a centralized marketing intelligence organization.

ING also introduced a detailed marketing campaign dashboard to monitor all campaigns via all channels on a daily basis. Results such as campaign response, sales and net present value (NPV) could be monitored through the entire sales funnel and available in one report. In summary the core changes were:

1 Each channel was connected to the centralized system.
2 Both marketing and sales people received extensive training.
3 Campaigns are now possible on a multi-channel or selective channel basis. Whereas ING's old campaign activity was exclusively based on outbound events such as direct mail, email and outbound call centre calls, the new program supports all marketing activities and enables staff to "market and sell" on inbound channels too – at the branches, on the bank's website and via inbound calls to the call centre.

4 Personalized marketing messages are now easy to do. Each customer can receive an individual product offer based on what's already known about them and what's been learnt during the recent interactions.
5 A continuous dialog can be maintained. By collecting customer responses from different channels and feeding them back into the data warehouse daily, the Bank can constantly optimize the offers made to customers.

To be able to achieve and deliver this transformational multi-channel change, the key lessons were:

1 Secure clear top-level sponsorship and support.
2 Involve stakeholders from multiple functions. ING set up a cross-functional project team that included people from customer intelligence, IT, marketing and all the different channels to collaborate on the effort from Day 1.
3 Prepare for organizational change. By far the biggest challenge of the project for ING was the organizational change that it required, resulting in a gradual shift of power and responsibility from the channels to marketing. A lot of training and education was required to overcome resistance to change from different parts of the organization – and this effort is still ongoing!
4 Expect a substantial operational effort. Running a centralized and continuous direct marketing program requires a lot of effort on a daily basis. Campaigns need to be monitored, new propositions need to be developed, and analytical models need to be created or refined. ING's customer intelligence team didn't initially expect that such an enormous level of effort would be required to do this effectively.

But the value and size of the prize are considerable. ING has increased average campaign response rates by an average of 60% while at the same time reducing its direct marketing costs by 35% per year. ROI and profitability have been transformed. ING feels it has now established the organization platform that can see the Bank through for the next 5 years.

* * * * *

The ING case has been examined in some detail because it shows that, while "the size of the prize" can be considerable, it does require time and a big and coordinated and multi-channel program of change. One thing that comes through loud and clear is that the days of the silo are well and truly over! Companies that continue to operate with functional silos will be especially vulnerable. The way a company organizes itself will be a critical facilitator.

McKinsey's 7-S Model

McKinsey has for many years been advocating a simple way of thinking about all these structural issues in its 7-S model (Figure 9).

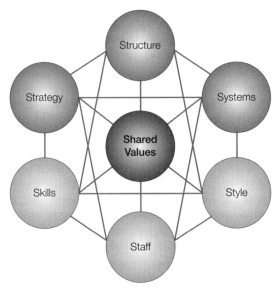

Figure 9   **The McKinsey 7-S model**

To deliver effective change, McKinsey research shows time and again that *all* of these seven factors need to be in alignment. The strategy must be backed up and reinforced by the way that the organization operates. The systems must enable and facilitate but must themselves be agile and flexible and be adaptable to new approaches and new ways of operating. Skills need to be developed and staff also need to be coached, helped and trained as to new ways of working. It's all very well to talk about the "multi-channel digital enterprise" but what does that really mean? What is really different from what we do today? Are we to be measured differently? Do we report to different people? If I'm a direct mail specialist, does this mean I'm redundant? Or does it mean I'm going to be retrained and given different responsibilities? Does MCE mean that my years of specialist know-how and expertise will still have a place and be valued, but that I'm now working in a broader customer context where I might become even more effective than I've been in the past?

It's instructive to review the journey that a number of companies have already made in working through just how best to organize and structure themselves for this multi-channel world.

A multi-channel approach

A multi-channel and integrated approach is now beginning to be recognized as the way forward:

1996 to 2001/02
Dedicated specialists

▷ New media
▷ Pioneering entrepreneurs
▷ Educators and informers

2003/04 to 2010
Silo

▷ Web 2.0 kicks in
▷ Sales become significant
▷ Separate teams

2011–
Multi-channel

▷ Recognition that the customer is multi-channel
▷ Need for consistent, coherent customer touch points

GUS plc

This is the story of how Great Universal Stores (GUS) structured e-commerce from 1998 to 2011.

In the early days, specialist web and e-commerce teams generally started out as separate departments, often reporting direct to the CEO with their own remit and dedicated staff. They often had their own premises which were sometimes deliberately set apart from the main office. It was a dot com mentality of: "This is so different we will separate it into a distinct business unit and then IPO the business for billions of dollars!" For example, John Lewis, the leading UK retail department store, at its peak had a separate team of nearly 200 e-commerce/web specialists in their own offices away from the main operation and for much of that time largely doing their own thing without recourse to the main stores group. And that was typical.

When I was e-commerce Director at Great Universal Stores through the Web 1.0 period, we quickly hired an e-commerce team, set up a separate unit called GUSCO.com which had its own offices away from each of the divisions (mainly Argos Retail, Experian and Burberry). Each of these core division's e-commerce businesses were technically taken out of their division, removed from the main business and put into GUSCO. There were plans to make add-on acquisitions and then separately IPO. We were given stock, not in the main listed company but in the new dot.com entity. On paper we were overnight dot.com millionaires (quickly to come to nothing!). But GUS were far from being the only major corporate that established this sort of structure. Reuters, at that time still separately quoted, did exactly the same. And others, like Time Warner, Dixons, Barclays Bank and N Brown with Zendor in the UK, all structured along similar lines.

Of course such moves and such separation caused much resentment across the rest of the organization. Why should this group get all the limelight? Why should they get separate options, what about us? Multi-channel collaboration was certainly not on the agenda at that time! And the whole concept of a digital-led corporate-wide transformation was also not up for discussion.

But when the bubble burst so all these structures collapsed. Many teams were disbanded, many superb business initiatives had to be shelved. I vividly recall a meeting in the City with a bunch of analysts who followed Great Universal Stores at that time. I was with the CEO of GUS, John Peace, who was a highly regarded City figure. But the analysts paid no respect to reputations. They were clear. The bubble had burst. And if GUS were to invest funds, any funds at all, in this "internet thing" then they would be obliged to conclude that the company lacked clear strategic direction so they would look to downgrade and mark down the share price.

Does this attitude demonstrate the short-term nature of stock markets? Or does it exemplify a lack of understanding as to how the world was changing? It mattered little, because GUS had first and foremost to manage its share price and protect shareholder value. It immediately meant the end of GUSCO.com, the end of that dream. And I remember John and I looking at each other and saying the same thing: "Well, that's the end of that!" – just a few words that summed up the end of the first internet revolution.

In GUS, the separate e-commerce team was cut and the staff housed elsewhere. Some, for example, went to Argos where they sat, miserable and isolated, labeled as "that webby person" who, it was assumed, was some kind of techy who could build you a website and not much else. From a reporting-line point of view, it was typically the IT department which then reluctantly assumed responsibility. And meantime, a few of the more adventurous souls in IT started to acquaint themselves with html and even persuaded their managers to attend a few courses!

Of course, things did not languish like that for long. "Behind the scenes", internet access was growing, the number of people using the Net each day was increasing and they were spending more time per visit. And when broadband started to become more widely available in 2004 the second internet wave began.

Suddenly Brands and companies in all sectors were finding there was interest in their web presence and criticism if they had a poor site. Simple brochureware was no longer sufficient.

This triggered the next round of organization structuring as companies were compelled to bring in the skills and people who could handle and manage this web channel. The structures that emerged were still separate but not in the GUSCO.com mould. This time around e-commerce specialists were formal members of the Marketing and IT departments, although they had their own small group of desks together! They were still identifiable, still slightly unusual, but a bit closer to the core team.

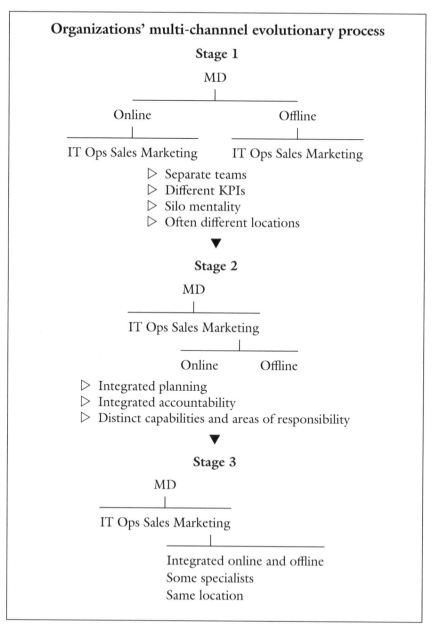

Organizations' multi-channnel evolutionary process

Stage 1

MD

Online   Offline

IT Ops Sales Marketing   IT Ops Sales Marketing

▷ Separate teams
▷ Different KPIs
▷ Silo mentality
▷ Often different locations

▼

Stage 2

MD

IT Ops Sales Marketing

Online   Offline

▷ Integrated planning
▷ Integrated accountability
▷ Distinct capabilities and areas of responsibility

▼

Stage 3

MD

IT Ops Sales Marketing

Integrated online and offline
Some specialists
Same location

The e-commerce team was better able to collaborate now. But even though reporting lines changed it would often still have its own budget, its own targets and goals and largely did its own thing. It was still small, revenues were growing fast but in absolute terms not huge and so "they could largely be left to their own devices." At the same time, the existence of an e-commerce team allowed the CEO to stand up at the AGM and talk briefly – in those days still very briefly – about their web strategy and show "a pretty screen shot of our website" (cue applause!).

So here we have, just five or six years ago in 2004/05/06, a still highly cynical business community. They could see an appetite for digital but were mostly unconvinced about how big it could become and how much investment it might need and how it might become the source of driving transformation just a few years later. And in keeping with that sentiment, they established a small web team with limited budgets, just enough to keep the website up and running,

But of course, since then, all the trends and growth rates have just multiplied and developed at significant rates. Companies have been *forced* to adapt, they have *had* to train up staff, recruit "digital talent", take on board new ideas, put online closer and closer to the centre, and get to Stage 3 of the organization structure. They have had to discover what skills they need to recruit, work out where to put those people, what responsibilities they should take, how to integrate that know-how so it becomes seamless and integrated, how to get the whole workforce to "think and act" as multi-channel managers, how to build that MCE and make it effective.

So with Great Universal Stores: how are they now structured to respond to and take advantage of this new era? Well, one thing for sure is that they have now had some 12 years' experience of trying different structures, finding out what worked and what failed and assessing what sort of solutions would fit best with their culture, ambitions and style of working. And the value of that experience should not be underestimated. All organization development is a journey and a series of evolutions, some of which work brilliantly and some of which need to be adjusted. People often ask: Why can't we be like XYZ Co, they seem to have solved this problem, they seem to be doing well, why can't we be like them? And the simple answer is that they may well, like Great Universal, have spent years of trial and error and migration and of taking series of steps. And another company can't just leap to that. Even if it could, it would likely amount to a revolution rather than an evolution and revolutions in companies are rarely successful. The staff, the style, the systems, the culture just can't adapt that quickly.

Great Universal as a company has demerged itself into three separate quoted companies: Home Retail Group (including Argos and Homebase), Experian and Burberry. Home Retail is by far the most developed multi-channel organization. They have developed substantial expertise along those lines. They have long-established their reputation for excellence in linking the web and bricks 'n mortar. "Click and Collect" followed fast on the heels of "Ring and Reserve" and customers are very used to the multiple ways of touching and interacting and researching and buying from the company.

Now the whole organization is multi-channel, and marketers and technical staff are expected, naturally and seamlessly, to take a full 360° rounded view of their complete set of channel and customer opportunities. There are some skill experts in Search Engine Marketing, Mobile and Social Media, for instance. That's simply because these areas are either new or require specialist skills and know-how. But in general, the organization is run collectively and collaboratively with no silos. And in the IT department, that integration is all the more advanced as they look to utilize internet-based technology solutions. All this means that the organization can still be confidently led on a traditional and proven functional basis. But those functions must now provide a fully-skilled 360° capability and should be able to provide a coherent and holistic and integrated and multi-channel solution.

* * * * *

And finally, if we want one more indication of the need for multi-channel change and the organization challenge that necessarily accompanies it, then here's a cautionary tale.

32% of people in an Econsultancy survey cited silo structures as *the* key barrier to digital progress in their company. And Andrew Walmsley, internet entrepreneur and commentator, tells this story about Barclays Bank. It had a Head of Digital who ran a digital team that controlled the website and were accountable for online sales. It also had a separate Marketing department which claimed to do all marketing and controlled the marketing budget. When it was decided who should control the online budget: why of course, it would be *in*appropriate to give that to the Head of Digital – budgets after all were the historic focus of all marketing departments! So the large Search Engine marketing budget of c. £10m was given to, yes, the Marketing department. But, at that time, they really knew very little about this area. They had no interest in Search. Their only metric was a cost one. Could they reduce the budget? And they did just that, dramatically. As a result the Bank's search engine presence became poor and mismanaged – such that a search for "sperm bank" would bring up a prominent listing for the bank. Online sales tumbled. And this saga took months to unfold, for people to stop laying blame and realize that quite simply some very basic structural mistakes were being made. Instead of everyone being measured collectively, the different teams were all measured on different things. The cost in lost opportunities was enormous.

Digital channels expose the real customer relationships and the way organizations do business as never before. Sadly these sorts of siloed situations are still commonplace. Business teams generally still have a long journey of change ahead to address these issues and stop the erosion of value.

13 Changes to the Workplace and in the Workforce

What will be the impact of digital transformation on the 2020 workplace? Will office life still be more or less the same, will we still have an office to go to, will we all need to become tech geeks and programmers, will be still be typing on Microsoft Word or will be talking to our computer and using VRS? Will we still meet and socialize with our co-workers and have office friends and networks or will we simply interact remotely? Will our remit be global or will we still act and think within local country boundaries? Will there still be specific function groups, for example for Marketing and IT, or will we all need to become multi-skilled, multi-channel experts?

For sure, the workplace will have changed and there are seven key themes that will characterize this change:

1 Mobile: meaning same speed instant screen access from anywhere
2 Anytime: 24/7/365 communication
3 Democratization: more people involved
4 Flatter hierarchies: less emphasis on managing downwards/upwards and more on contribution and engagement
5 The "Knowledge worker"
6 Global: no boundaries
7 Automation: a lot of what we do today will be done automatically by machines.

Let's consider each of these:

1 *Mobile*
At Unilever, as in almost every other organization, the culture and expectation used to be that people would come to work. They would clock-in or register or at least make their presence felt and be available. Today, Unilever's policy has shifted to accommodate three types of employee: resident, mobile and offsite. Residents are those who still come to work and have their own desk and workspace. That might be the Office manager, Security staff and others who prefer that style. The Mobile worker has typically been the Sales-person out and about with customers but returning to base and hot-desking

there, someone with access but no "permanent home". And then there is the remote worker, who may never visit the office, may be established at home or work as a connected contractor or consultant or supplier who needs and gets access to fellow employees, office news and information, email etc. but always from a remote station.

While that may be a simple but very appropriate way to think about the workplace in 2011, Unilever are studying how the next 10 years will change that categorization. One thing they are certain about: there will still be a need for an office, but there will be a substantial shift from resident to mobile and offsite. This has a far-reaching impact on the size and amount of office space required. It also, and most especially, impacts the IT and communications systems that enable people to still work effectively in teams and make informed and pragmatic decisions while perhaps never meeting in person. Unilever's challenge is that most of their employees like coming to work. They enjoy the learning and stimulation of working with colleagues as well as the social interaction. The advent of digital technology may allow companies such as Unilever to find new ways of working and collaborating, but it will also result in a different type of "office life".

The trend to mobile and offsite will continue to grow, but it may be driven as much by pressures to continue to reduce costs as by the availability of technology and what it can easily enable. This raises one stark question for the commercial property industry: Will we still need the same amount of office space in 2020? Surely, companies will be reviewing just how many people they really do need to house in the future. If a persuasive business and HR case can be made for encouraging mobile and offsite then it will be accompanied by the need for fewer square feet. That might impact the major business centers less than the secondary ones. Companies might still feel they "need a presence in the City", for example, but business parks in secondary and tertiary locations may well struggle to retain occupancy rates.

This physical space dilemma is no different than the one facing retail organizations, discussed in Chapter 11. As online shopping becomes more and more attractive and easy, retailers will need fewer shops. And only now, after years of the "doom mongers" saying that there is a real estate time bomb waiting to go off, are retailers truly beginning to review their shop portfolio and space needs over the next 10 years. Such are the lead times that it can easily take up to 10 years from design to build to occupancy. If the future does require less physical office space then it may soon be time to sell stock in commercial property developers!

2   *Anytime*

The ubiquity of computers and mobile devices will increase expectations of immediate interaction and response. Consumers already expect 24/7/365 access to the internet, to online shopping (ever seen a website notice saying it is closed for the weekend!), to call centers to get technical support whenever needed, access to bank accounts and money transfers, the availability of advice and service whenever they want it and wherever they are. As that consumer demand continues to grow, all forms of customer service will need to provide round-the-clock support. Gone will be the days that people will accept "Our office hours are 9 to 5 Monday till Friday".

Metro Bank is just one of the new organizations to recognize this. It has been a pioneer in retail banking, offering 7-day-week branch opening hours, 8 till 8. Will we, for example, see other financial institutions follow suit? Most have now recovered from the 2008 banking crisis and have, frustratingly, reverted to their old ways, shored up by strongly recovering profits. No need or urgency to change perhaps? But, for example, 24/7 screen trading could allow stock markets to function at all hours. Why do we still need the ceremonial bell to signal the beginning and end of a day's trading? Global trading already means that a stock can be traded even when a particular market has closed. Likely consolidations of the London market with Toronto and the NYSE with Deutsche Bourse, and the 2011 announcement that the Hong Kong exchange is looking to find a global merger partner ... all herald some transformational changes that may well lead one day to one global stock market operating 24/7/365.

If stock trading can go this way, then what other parts of the banking process might also change? And if these changes follow through, they may become part of a universal trend to offer a continuous "we never close" service and facility.

And all that means that the workforce will need to adapt to that pattern. It's already happened in retail with some stores open 24 hours a day and, of course, the manufacturing sector, with its high fixed cost asset base, long ago implemented 24/7 shift patterns and working practices to leverage that cost base and investment.

In today's world of competitiveness, the end of the "job for life" philosophy, cost and other pressures, few jobs are truly "safe" and the workforce has had to become more adaptable and flexible to keep its jobs and its wages. So accepting shift patterns, having a willingness to work "nights" while having the day off, participating in global teams and ventures which may conflict with historic social/relaxation at home with family patterns, may become more widely adopted and accepted as the normal way of doing business and holding down a job. In fact most managers today, especially if they are involved in a global company, find they have to have a huge amount of 24/7 flexibility. Time zones mean that a US company dealing with a partner organization or colleagues working in China has only a limited window of same-day time to set up video and conference calls. If a manager in San Francisco wanted to speak to a colleague in Shanghai on the same day then that call would have to be no later realistically than 06.00 PST because the time in Shanghai, at 16 hours ahead, would be 22.00. And it's becoming increasingly common for execs who want to have a "quiet chat" with a colleague or investor or recruit away from the rush of the day job to book conference calls during the weekend.

A Gartner report looking at the 2020 workplace makes this prediction: "Many [employees] will have neither a company-provided physical office nor a desk, and their work will increasingly happen 24 hours a day, seven days a week. In this work environment, the lines between personal, professional, social and family matters ... will disappear."

3   Democratization

The 2011 McKinsey report on Web 2.0 found that companies who actively encourage wide-spread internal and social networking were more successful than those that did not. The report identified twelve specific web networking technology tools which could contribute to make that difference. These included:

> *blogs, mash-ups (applications that, for example, combine multiple sources of data into a single tool), microblogging, peer to peer, podcasts, prediction markets ("the wisdom of crowds"), rating, RSS (Really Simple Syndication), social networking, tagging, video sharing and wikis.*

Encouraging this internal sharing, discussion, collaboration and up-to-date communication was found to produce benefits in a number of areas. Increased employee satisfaction was near the top of the list as employees were discovering new ways to contribute and feel part of a community with a shared purpose. And the company found benefits in reduced operating costs and an increasing number of successful innovations to the working practices resulting in increased speed of decision-making and faster time to market.

It sounds like this is the way all companies should be moving: a demonstrable and proven way to make a company work in a digital environment; benefits to both employee and employer; potentially easy to implement even though many companies might struggle without a unified messaging and collaboration platform, disparate systems, no connected-up intranet, firewalls or policies restricting access to the worldwide web or to social networks specifically. But at the end of the day they don't need much more than a web browser and a password-protected environment. And there are companies who are already out there and making this Web 2.0 internal socializing work.

Dresdner Bank uses an internal knowledge-sharing "socialtext wiki" to manage meeting agendas and capture the key points and conclusions to provide an easily accessible record and archive trail of project progress which is open to all. Dell has an active social networking program that reaches out to customers but also seeks to engage internally to help unify a geographically diverse global workforce. And instead of waiting for the next CEO podcast, everyone is encouraged to blog, to set up their own community groups, whether work-related or not, and to participate in discussion forums. Walt Disney, Oracle/Sun Microsystems and even General Motors are finding these techniques valuable in both communicating their own corporate messages and also giving everyone in the company a voice and, most importantly, a channel to be heard.

This is the digital equivalent of the water cooler conversation. It's been heralded as one of the biggest changes in a century in the way companies organize and communicate internally. While much was made of the intranet, it typically relied on corporate IT to establish some unnecessarily complex solution which took 2 years to build, cost millions, didn't work well, had an appalling user interface and which no one used. This time around web technology makes it easy: the interface can be simple, Facebook can be the template, keep it hosted in the cloud, adopt a standard keyword search facility and let the users populate and paint the space. A recent piece of Forrester research on the subject observed that the product or process is owned by all the people who create it, wherever they are in the creation process, and that drives a collective sense of ownership and responsibility.

4 *Flatter hierarchies*

The classic hierarchical organization structure is not fit for the 2020 work place. The new technology world, and the tech socials who will drive it, will require a more collaborative and cooperative way of working. "Command and Control" hierarchy will need to give way to "Autonomy and Empowerment". Looser team-based designs will need to be adopted to replace today's multi-layered approach in which we often find managers managing managers!

As Charles Handy, one of the great strategists of recent times has pointed out: "There is no logic which says that this ... decision sequence needs to be turned into a vertical ladder so that those who take the necessary earlier decisions are higher in the hierarchy than those who implement them. That is where history comes in, for those who got there first obviously set things up this way." And the larger the organization the more complex the hierarchy and the greater the bureaucracy.

"Destructured" organization design is now being recognized as a form more suited to a fast-paced competitive environment which needs to be able to adapt quickly, make more immediate decisions and better harness the skills and expertise of the *whole* workforce. The buzz words are all about "flexibility, speed, integration and innovation". And the magic number is 50.

50 is regarded as the size of structure and team where everyone can know everyone else, where it's possible to establish critical mass in terms of the variety of skills and experience, where people can easily communicate and collaborate, where decision-making can be quick, where "office politics" can be kept to a minimum and where a true sense of collective ownership can be fostered. Structure can be kept to small teams and team leaders where there is less emphasis on managing and more on doing and contributing. This can generate a sense of empowerment and a feeling that each person is responsible. It's no longer about "I did my bit", but more about "This is mine and we've all got to get it right!"

And yes, this may sound somewhat Utopian and the many who are involved today in a large corporate with all its established structures and ways of working may wonder how it is possible to migrate from the current to the new. But the forces for change will come both externally from the market place and the need to be competitive and also internally from the new generation of the workforce who will be making their own imprint on how they work and how best to organize.

HP, Xerox, General Electric are examples of big companies who have nevertheless been pioneers of flatter structures. GE was the archetype of the top-down, command-and-control structured company. But they have found ways to re-design their structure so that the divisions run as smaller entrepreneurial units. One of their techniques was to introduce "boundaryless management". This was a direct and persistent attack on their traditional vertical structure. Motorola, before restructuring, had 12 layers of management. After restructuring, it had considerably fewer. By proceeding cautiously, it managed its transition in a way that still protected the company's reputation as a good employer. Edward Jones, the US stockbroker, moved to make itself a flat company by structuring as a confederation of autonomous entrepreneurial units. They are nevertheless still bound together by a central set of shared core values and service ethics. The company today is a network of brokers, each of which works from their own remote but connected office. Companies like Apple and Google are leaders among the new wave who have built their foundations on these same principles. It is becoming the preferred way of working for the new breed of tech companies who have the flexibility and agility to embrace digital technology in this changing landscape.

5   The Knowledge worker

The great business guru Peter Drucker succinctly described the fundamental shift brought about by the last 10 to 15 years of technology revolution:

> In fact, knowledge is the only meaningful resource today. The traditional "factors of production" – land, labor and capital – have not disappeared, but they have become secondary. They can be obtained, and obtained easily, provided there is knowledge. And knowledge in this new sense means knowledge as a utility, knowledge as the new means to obtain social and economic results. (*Post-Capitalist Society*, 1993)

Knowledge has become power and it is estimated that more than 1.5 trillion dollars (GigaOm) a year is being invested worldwide in developing new information and communication technologies, software and hardware to exploit knowledge as a driving source of innovation and advantage. It is also estimated that in developed countries three-quarters of the workforce can now be categorized as being involved in knowledge work or service. (Forty years ago that fraction would have been about one-third.)

The implications are far-reaching for the type of work environment and for the skills people need. Digital knowledge capture, sharing and insight will become the new order. Traditional tasks will become automated, software will carry out the routine and commodity functions, workflow process will be managed by digital communications, paper will eventually become peripheral and people will become displaced and dispersed as a more virtual world of remote information and know-how take over. The interactions of knowledge work are shown in Figure 10.

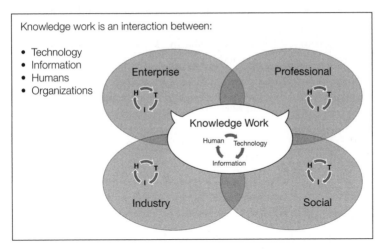

Figure 10 **Knowledge work components**
Source: PARC, Mark Bernstein

This future places a whole new emphasis on "organization design" and training and how to manage and get the best out of teams. "Knowledge workers" have become the new champions of the workforce and *Computer Weekly* has dubbed them the "new elite". Those who understand the technology, who are technically literate themselves, who know the basics of architecture and programming, who are up-to-speed with latest software and hardware in so far as it relates to their industry, who have an awareness of how the technology environment around them will evolve, whose understanding is intuitive enough that they can make the technology work for them, rather than be subjected to it ... these are the sorts of people who may well deserve to be called the "elite" in this decade. Some people grow up with an innate affinity to technology and to IT generally, others will need to be trained in and learn the requisite skills. Whether a salesperson or a marketer, a finance controller or an analyst, corporate careers will need to be built on a thorough understanding of digital technology and how to leverage and harness the knowledge and insight that can be derived from it.

Xerox embarked on a knowledge project to capture the know-how and expertise of their 25,000 strong service technician workforce that was based all over the world. They realized that so much knowledge and know-how was left with the individual that a lot of expertise was being lost and a huge amount of duplication and time was being invested in working out answers to the same problems. Extensive documentation was, it was felt, not the answer because their research showed that most technicians could fix most problems. Instead it was the unexpected and the unpredictable that caused delay and customer, as well as technician, frustration.

Xerox's research centre in Palo Alto, PARC, set about working on a new technology solution based around the idea of establishing a social or "water-cooler" network where the shared gossip and experience could be captured and easily accessed. Through multiple field observations and design-testing, PARC scientists developed a knowledge-sharing system that codified technicians' tacit know-how, lessons learned, tips and ideas.

It was recognized that to make this work, the technology environment that was created had to be "90% a social process", that its use would evolve over time, that technicians would need to be trained into the process, how to use it and how to input to it. The aim was to create an intelligent work space that users could adapt and take from it what would be helpful so it became a part of their natural process and interactions. The environment was tested "in different organizational settings given the socio-cultural factors of technology use and adoption."

6   Global – no boundaries

A recent PWC report has been examining the increasingly global nature of the economy. Their key conclusions are no surprise. The world is "getting smaller", 25% of the global workforce is expected to be based in India and a further 20% in China by 2050. The aging population in developed countries means one-third of the workforce there will be over 50 with the possibility that leadership in technology and innovation will shift to a younger, more entrepreneurial Asian business community. Cultural and language barriers will continue to decline as social and community networking becomes further established and entrenched. Trade tariffs and other artificial barriers will become harder to maintain and senior business leaders will have to have the confidence and skills to step outside geographic and other boundaries and embrace the "global village".

The biggest challenge, as already touched upon, is that work can be done anywhere. This does not just mean outside the office at home, but in any country anywhere that has adequate communication connections. And the advent of Cloud computing simply reinforces this trend. In a recent review the *Economist* described how, just as servers, storage and desktops are becoming a "virtual cloud", so we are moving to a point where the labor element of IT will also start to become "virtualized". Combine this with a universal skills vocabulary, a universal business language and lower wage costs and we quickly get to a scenario where to keep their jobs the workforce will potentially have to be especially flexible and adaptable, willing to learn but also potentially ready to locate to wherever the knowledge centers of excellence are based.

Of course the "exodus" of jobs from West to East, the brain drain, the growing power of Asian economies, the lower wage rates, the entrepreneurial spirit which is already strong in the developing economies, and Brazil, Russia, India and China in particular, has been well-documented. Armageddon scenarios have been variously touted and rehearsed, predicting massive unemployment and declining economic prospects among Western countries. But those scenarios have been around for some time and we are still yet to see any substantial impact other than slow and incremental change while in

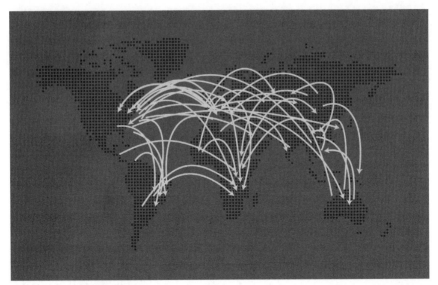

Figure 11 **Job migration**

fact the major global innovators are still being born out of the west coast of the US, just as they have been for the past 30 years.

What has shifted fundamentally is the mindset required to operate effectively. It has to be global and strategies which are only local in scope are potentially missing big opportunities. That is going to be a key part of the competitive landscape through till 2020 – envisaging and identifying how to scale a new initiative quickly across the world while it is fresh and innovative and different and before it's copied and reengineered by countless others. The new entrepreneurs of the day are coming to market with this way of thinking. The world of boundaries and borders just does not exist. If we can quickly and easily participate in a virtual game with someone in China then why can't we just as easily do business together as well?

7 *Automation*

Is automation a job killer or a job creator? The international market for automation-related products is estimated at c. €300 billion according to Forbes, and growth is estimated at 6% to 10% per annum. In Germany, for example, that translates into a €35 billion market place employing some 230,000 people. It has become a major contributor to Germany's electronics industry. It has become so wide-spread that it actually reinforces the attractiveness of Germany as a top industrial location, encouraging new companies to set up both domestically and from overseas and all establishing new jobs. Inevitably the skill requirements for these companies require a good to high degree of technology literacy but every organization needs people at all levels to make things happen. In fact so important is this industry as a job creator that it attracts high-level political and state support.

However technology-based industries do not typically promise the same number of local jobs as asset-based production or retail businesses. Compare Google with McDonald's, companies with similar overall revenues. McDonald's employs some 400,000 people worldwide, revenue per average worker of c. $60,000. Google however employs around 25,000 people at average revenue of c. $1m each. The question is: What if McDonald's were to become more like Google because of the level of production automation it was able to introduce? Would it keep the same number of employees but shift the work focus to other areas of value-add and customer service? Or would it simply reduce the number of people on its payroll?

A Gartner 2020 study considered that the worst case scenario would be characterized by substantial broad-based structural unemployment as machines do more and more of the work that was previously done by people. To avoid such a situation, the Gartner research highlighted that the need for flexibility and adaptability among the workforce would be key. Moving to where the work is, being ready to reskill and learn new methods and applications, working to contract rather than having a job for life, part-time instead of full-time, working remotely and not in an office, working for small independent companies rather than big institutions (as the smaller organization takes advantage of the cloud to harness numerous remote supporting technologies and partnerships), self-improvement to continue to learn and develop ... all these things will become part of the 2020 work scene. And with it our schools and universities will urgently need to adapt their courses to have an increasing vocational and pragmatic rather than academic output.

* * * * *

Let's leave the final word on the changing workplace to Philip Tidd, a partner at DEGW, the global strategy consultancy. He argues that by 2020 we will be able to say: "Work has left the building." He goes on to say that:

> Synchronicity and co-location are being turned on their head by new generations and new technology. People will no longer need to be in the same place at the same time every day. We will still need the office, but the office will be different as technology and the way we work changes. We will connect virtually.

We know that the way we interact and depend upon computers will experience a step change. What we don't know is how quickly it will happen, or what all the consequences will be.

14   The Digital Divide

While much as the world focuses on the rapid growth of the internet, the number of online connections, the advent of smart phones, e-commerce and social networking, there is an often-forgotten story. That is the digital divide (Plate 10). While many countries are racing to improve infrastructure, broadband speed and provide government support to develop their digital world, those without the same resources are languishing.

Comparing the "most switched on" countries to the least, there is a widening gap, as shown in Figure 12.

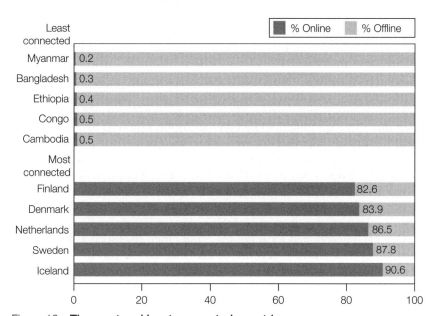

Figure 12   **The most and least connected countries**
Source: ITU.

The scale of a country's digital "readiness" and infrastructure clearly reflects the state of its economy. The *Economist* identified factors such as how organized is the local business community, what is the social and cultural environment to drive demand, the sophistication of the legal environment to make connectivity safe and the local Government's own set of priorities and vision.

In Finland, near the top of the table, with only around 17% of the population unconnected, the Government has declared "digital inclusion" to be a basic human right. It expects that everyone will be internet-enabled by 2012. Its public libraries have become centers of excellence with open internet access, laptop "doctors" who can fix technical problems and continuous training available. Greece, on the other hand, sits at the bottom of the European league table and the *Economist* report highlights the significant dispersed rural population outside of the few big cities, relatively low average income levels and poorer education standards. In the US, usually held up as the best-connected country, there are digital divides too. A study by NAF found that less than 10% of Native Americans had internet access. "Tribal homelands have stood like barren deserts in pockets across the technology-rich lands of the United States."

The mobile phone is proving to be the great solution. It doesn't need government support and it doesn't need a fixed line infrastructure, it simply needs consumer interest and demand. As many reports are now demonstrating, the mobile phone is turning into Africa's "silver bullet". The *Guardian* recently commented that, despite "bone-rattling roads, unavailable banks, unaffordable teachers, unmet medical need," the mobile phone is transforming the lives of millions of Africans and Asians who are fed up with waiting for their Governments to provide better infrastructure (Plate 11).

There are now some 4 billion mobile subscriptions worldwide and in the developing nations it means that people who've never had a landline or owned a car or even a bicycle now own a mobile. Mobile phones have very quickly become a fixture in even the poorest parts of the world and it's estimated that there are some 250 million subscriptions now in Africa. So widespread has this become that charity workers are finding that people are prepared to forgo food and clothing to have their own mobile. The director of Earth Institute notes that it has already become an indispensable accessory.

Initially it was feared that access would be severely limited, simply by the absence of a mobile phone network but that gap has also been filled surprisingly rapidly with the likes of Vodafone, France Telecom, local operators like Gambia Telecom and local not-for-profit enterprises such as Kiwanja all contributing to a growing network of masts across the continent. Business has stepped in where Government was unwilling or unable and has begun to establish country-wide connections which are transforming lives. "If this had been an EU or OECD or World Bank initiative then it's doubtful we'd be where we are today, but mobile network operators can see a very good business model here."

Success has come because even the poorest are turning to the phone for help. Villagers in rural areas are now calling for a doctor or an ambulance (if they are not too far away), people with AIDS are seeking advice, farmers and fishermen can now find the best market prices. Mobile banking is becoming very popular with people using their mobiles to transfer money and make payments, usually by sending a text message. M-Pesa was one of the early pioneers in Kenya, attracting some 5 million customers and providing

branchless banking. The early system did have its faults
but it's now run by a joint
venture between IBM and
Vodafone and proving indispensable for sending money
to far-flung relatives, paying
bills and even for the taxi
home. Users just register at a
local store which has applied

Source: BBC Pictures, BBC Photo Library

to become part of the M-Pesa virtual banking community. The store could
be a nearby petrol station. Users load money onto their phone, send a text
to a third party who takes their phone into their nearest store where they can
collect the cash. Participating stores manage monthly e-float accounts and
have access to M-Pesa agents to sort out their cash balances.

Mobile phone penetration in developing countries now stands at 68%
according to the latest report from the ITU. That is higher than any other
technology before. Prices are falling and in many remote communities the
phone is a shared access device providing connections for many more than
the actual subscriber. However internet connectivity is far less available and
fast speed broadband is some way away. That may not matter in a remote area
where simple voice and SMS will meet a range of immediate needs. But for
example, those in the education sector see huge opportunities for e-learning
if only higher bandwidth and speed were available. As all the research has
shown with regard to the internet, it's a truism to say, "build it and they
will come". Where mobile internet access has been made available, usage
and pages viewed has taken off and the amount of mobile data consumed in
African markets matches the amount in developed countries.

Satellite is offering an alternative way to bridge the digital divide. At the
end of 2010 the Avanti HYLAS 1 satellite was launched in Europe. For the
first time it enables an interactive broadband service targeted at some 20
countries across Europe. Previous satellite solutions had required a separate
back channel over a phone line for the interactive component. But the new
Avanti uses the Ka-band which provides the back channel through the satellite. BT has subsequently announced that it will use the Avanti service to
provide broadband via satellite to black spots in south-west England which
have no broadband access. It's estimated that there are still some 20 million
homes in Europe with no broadband at all, so this could be the speeded-up
route that provides that access. While this satellite is not as fast as "ground-
based" solutions and probably will still not enable VOD or large-scale data
transfer, it is claimed to be "more than adequate for average daily use".

Meantime back in Africa, more promises have been made about delivering internet connections. A consortium of the World Bank, the African
Development Bank and the ITU have said they will find the funding to connect all major cities to broadband by 2012. This includes major projects like
laying a fiber optic cable along the east coast from Durban all the way up

to Port Sudan at a cost of c. $200m. If this cable network is built it would connect 21 African countries, enable thousands of businesses and millions of people to get online, and probably at much lower prices than they would have to pay today. Though the original investment costs do keep growing part of this project has already gone live up to Kenya and it is still on track for its 2012 completion.

So while the digital divide certainly exists today, even the "excluded" are finding ways to connect. Some governments may be slow to provide infrastructure but private business investment is stepping into the gaps. It is clear that people everywhere do want the technology. Their use of it may be different, many will use the mobile phone instead of cable or phone line, some may have to wait a while for the touch-and-go cheap access that many in the West are getting used to with their smart phones, some will use it for emergency contact or self improvement while others will just casually browse and surf, but the momentum for closing the divide and providing universal high speed access is unstoppable.

15 Case Study: Building a Successful Online Business

Three key questions drive this chapter:

1 What's required to build a growing, profitable and sustainable online business?
2 What marks out the winners?
3 What are the lessons learnt?

We can look at a number of outstanding case studies. Some products and services will lend themselves naturally and easily to online marketing and selling. Others can be harder to establish. But what comes through clearly is that there are no barriers. There is no reason why any brand or business organization, no matter what sector it competes in, cannot achieve significant growth through online channels.

In the first edition of *e-Shock* in Web 1.0 days, readers showed considerable interest in what was called the "e-test". It looked at a brand's basic characteristics and identified a "propensity score". Brands with high scores were considered to have a high likelihood of online success, and if you got those high scores then you knew you needed to act immediately! These typically included products that could be simply presented in 2D on a page and where the purchase decision was based on an intelligent assessment of factors like price and availability. So services, like buying insurance and airline tickets, and simple-to-present products, like books, CDs and DVDs, could immediately be identified. You didn't really need to visit a shop or meet someone to evaluate whether this was a product you would like to buy, especially if you knew already what you wanted. But what if your sector got a low "propensity score"? Did that mean no customer interest in online communications and sales?

The purpose of this section is to review a number of case studies, to check whether "propensity scores" still matter and to look at the key lessons learnt to get some potential tips for future success.

Case Study 1: TripAdvisor

On TripAdvisor you can book flights, hotels and restaurants. It provides coverage of every major destination across the globe. It will check other travel intermediaries like Expedia, Opodo, Orbitz, eDreams and consolidate the information from every airline for the designated departure airport flying to any destination, for example. And the search engine is operating increasingly closely to real time (though data updates vary depending on real-time news feeds from each airline). The amount of data being crunched in each search is considerable and yet it's done in just a few seconds. What's more, it provides reviews, ratings, testimonials from consumers, search comparison by price, by time, by airline, by date. There are also search alerts so you can be told about availability or relevant news updates. You can link in via Facebook so you and your pals could book online together. You can also access the site in specially configured form via your mobile, and you can search for a local hotel (the site can identify via GPS on your mobile where you are so, for example, you could type "find me nearest accommodation"), compare reviews and Book Now! It now operates in 14 languages across 23 countries worldwide and covers 24,000 destinations, attracting 40 million visitors each month.

And when was TripAdvisor first launched? In 2000 – at the time when Web 1.0 was bust, when the internet bubble was bursting, when doomsayers were saying there was no future for businesses on the internet, when naysayers (like my friends at Argos at that time!), even if they could acknowledge the consumer convenience and benefits, would never invest anything significant.

What the founders of TripAdvisor have demonstrated is *how* you can build a substantial business on the Net. They aimed to become the "category killer". They wanted to be the destination brand that everyone went to. They asked, "How can we be that 'first port of call'?" They found backers in Flagship Ventures in Cambridge, Mass, in 2000 who were themselves passionate about online and believed in its long-term potential. The backers gave the management team the time and the commitment to build a technically complex and demanding website environment that could manage the huge number of real-time data feeds and align that with a sophisticated search engine. What TripAdvisor does today has become more commonplace and easier to achieve, but it does still take a lot of time, commitment and ingenuity to get there.

Payback came in 2005 with the sale to IDC who immediately put TripAdvisor together with Expedia. IDC have continued to invest and reports suggest they have put in a further $350m to get the site to a global, multi-country scale. In 2010 it reported profits of close to $200m and it was expecting continued high levels of growth as it neatly mixes social comment, advice and recommendations with an easy-to-use booking reference engine. Latest conservative valuations put it at more than $1bn though that places no value yet on the "social community" aspects and its continuing ability to attract millions of visitors, its brand name or its category-killing status.

Case Study 2: Amazon

Why have they been so successful? There are three key reasons:

(i) First and foremost it's a simple, single-minded idea and highly utilitarian. Type in the name of a book, film, music etc. and up comes a ranked list. The format and presentation has hardly changed since it first launched.

(ii) It's very very easy to use. One click and you can buy. You can complete a transaction in seconds. This functionality is exactly what internet buyers are looking for. The general internet mantra is "quick, easy and convenient". If a site experience can pass that test then it's got the core platform to succeed. Sounds straightforward, where's the complexity of that? But how many other sites offer one-click functionality? They will  ask you to log-in, remember your user name and password and often expect you to complete all the credit card details all over again. And even if you can get through that then you are often shunted off to some Visa verification site where you're expected to remember yet another password. But hang on, I've visited and bought from this site before, why can't they be like Amazon and just remember me?

The more clicks the visitor has to make to complete a purchase the more likely it is that they will not complete and will abandon the shopping cart. Abandon rates are typically between 40% and 80%, which is already alarmingly high. How do you manage to lose a customer who has got that far into the process? They liked what they saw, selected it, got ready to buy it and then 40% to 80% drop out! With Amazon one-click, you can see how that loss is minimized. One click and they've already bought! But research shows that after more than 3 clicks consumers start to get frustrated, after 6 clicks there are significantly diminishing returns and after 12 clicks, the rate of abandon quickly hits the 80%-plus mark.

So why would anyone design a click-heavy site? Extraordinarily, in this fast changing and competitive landscape, Amazon still stand out a mile in this respect. Not surprisingly, they have seen off usurpers like booksellers Waterstones and Borders outside of the US, and media company Bertelsmann's Bol.com, all of which have flirted and tried to compete with Amazon's core book product line and failed to grab any significant market share.

"Easy to use" should be something every site now scores well on. But they don't. 2010 saw another long list of "worst websites". According to the annual "websites that suck" awards, bad sites ranged from ShopinParadise.com (which is so wallpapered with content that it's almost impossible to read) to Yale School of Art (Art.Yale.edu), which you might have hoped would have inspired artistically or aesthetically in some way and Zinc Bistro in Scottsdale, US. Their site launches with an extremely annoying soundtrack and then shows no map information about where it is or how to book a table. There's no site nav and the tiny navigation link at the foot of the page does not work. It might be the greatest restaurant/bar in the world but you wouldn't be able to easily find it or eat there. What's the point? How much business are they losing? Who is the site designer that put this together and thought this was a good idea? Who paid for it and why did they not ask a few fairly simple and obvious questions? Why does this happen? Why do the obvious mistakes keep occurring?

(iii) The third test is that the "page must load immediately" (and countless research reports from Forrester make this point). Why is this so important? According to Forrester:

▷ 57% of consumers will abandon a website if the page does not load within 3 seconds.
▷ Estimates are that a company can lose c. 50% of its potential online sales if its pages don't load quickly.
▷ For every second of delay in page loading, the viewer will spend less time looking at the page once it does load and, in particular, will not absorb any secondary promotional content or links.

Case Study 3: MyFaveShop.com

A few years ago, I observed at first hand a new e-commerce venture which became called MyFaveShop.com. The idea could be described as follows:

It was all about "social shopping". As you browsed the web you could click on anything you liked. It might be an item of clothing, an intended present, a Xmas list. Instead of that appearing in a long Favorites list, you could capture the image and the product detail and put that into your own specially designed shop. You could then invite friends to see your "collection", all laid out in a 3D-like retail store environment. And you could decorate and furnish that store in your own style (see Plate 12).

You could, say, put together a group of 4 or 5 dresses or coats you liked and had plans to buy one for the season. You could invite your friends to look at them and get their opinion on what would suit you best. And then, if you wanted you could click and buy.

The core idea was "shopping together", co-browsing so you could look at the same screen together remotely in real time. (For example, you could ask your sister Edith in Australia if she thinks this dress would suit Mum currently wintering in sunny Florida!)

But however nice the idea, it has taken three paragraphs and a picture to describe. And therein lies its complexity. In contrast, Amazon takes one very short sentence to define: look at a list of products, select and buy. MyFave-Shop involved a lot of ideas and messages and, because it was new and there was nothing like it at the time to benchmark or compare it to, required a lot of explanation for people visiting the site for the first time. How could you define in one short sentence what this was about?

So things got complicated when it came to developing the simple, easy-to-use website and navigation. There were a variety of messages and explanations and illustrations all vying for prominence on the home page. Each member of the team had their own judgment on the order and the priorities. The investors had their own marked preferences too. And even the consumer research that was conducted proved inconclusive. Some liked the idea, others didn't and each picked up on different aspects of the proposition:

▷ "I like the idea of social shopping"
▷ "Design your own shop...that's cool"
▷ "Put all my favorite things in one place"
▷ "Create a wish list of things I want"
▷ "Looking together at the same screen"
▷ "I like the choice of shop designs and being able to paint and furnish it how I like"

To complicate things further, it was clear that some visitors to the site would be web-savvy and would "get" the concept quickly, need little hand-holding and want to get on with the site experience. Ohers would need more show-and-tell and so require an introduction and explanation. And finally, there had quite clearly to be an income stream, so it was important that visitors got the message that they could buy as well as browse. At the same time, space had to be found to incorporate key ad messages from brands!

The web team started to get very bogged down in the detail and with trying to find the right web experience. Does the home page lead with the introductory explanation and even a step-by-step video or does it offer a navigation which tries to tempt all the different types of users and visitors? And what about repeat visitors? How to get them engaged enough to register in the first instance? What type of data capture should be requested? At what stage in the visit is registration best requested?

The website did launch, struggled out of Beta and was eventually and somewhat mercifully sold to another e-commerce organization for a price that at least gave some return. The new owners themselves found that they were gradually forced to simplify things and in the end it became more and more like any other shopping website.

MyFaveShop's failure was a shame because there were some great ideas here. If the messaging challenge had been solved, if the right prioritization had been found, if the user experience had been put together in a simple and easy-to-use form, if the investors had had more patience (or is that indulgence?), if the team had been able to cut through the complexity and, for example, found a way to start with just one big idea while adding other complementary messages and functions later, then this could, perhaps, have been a winning website. But the lessons from a disappointing experience can be just as compelling as ones about a successful one!

Simplicity is without doubt a virtue when it comes to designing websites, content for mobile, Apple apps or any other stuff for a screen. That "home page" is a small piece of real estate: it's precious, the people who look at it are typically impatient and expect something quick, easy-to-digest, intuitive and arranged in such a way that they can very very easily make a decision to invest in this experience or click away. Most websites have overall "fall-off rates" of over 90% from their home page. In other words, most visitors never make it to Page 2. Why have Google and Facebook been so quick to catch on? While there may be many reasons, part of the explanation lies in their beautiful simplicity. You know immediately and unequivocally what they are all about.

Why is user experience simplicity so crucial? Research from Forrester and others highlights the following:

▷ Most people will leave if they cannot immediately (within 3 seconds) understand what the site was about.
▷ 8 out of 10 people will not revisit a site after a disappointing experience.
▷ 35% of those who did have a disappointing experience say they will proactively tell friends not to visit that site.

▷ Research from the Aberdeen Group shows that a 1-second delay in page load times equals 11% fewer page views, a 16% decrease in visitor satisfaction and a 7% loss in conversion. And, as an example, Shopzilla improved average page load times from 6 seconds to 1.23 seconds and experienced a 25% increase in page views and a 12% increase in revenues.

▷ More than 60% of mobile users who visited brand websites, found that mobile access was slow and information on the screen was cluttered and sometimes unreadable.

Case Study 4: General Motors

According to *PC* magazine, 58% of people research a product or service provider online before buying. In the auto sector that percentage goes up to 82% according to AutoTrader. Buying a car is a complex decision-making process as buyers compare and contrast models, review specs, read brochures, look at video content showcasing the car and the driving experience, and that's well before they've visited the showroom. Further research has shown that the auto sector is unlike other high ticket-value items. With, say, the purchase of a new TV set, consumers will use online to narrow their choice down to a couple of different brands/models, for example, the "Sony Bravia" and the "Samsung 654 LCD". With research into cars, however, people will use online to decide which brand they are going to buy and they will prioritize one only, for example, "I'm going to buy a Ford", and then will have in mind, at most, a couple of different model options. So online is even more critical in the auto sector. Make the online experience compelling and you drive your prospective customer right to your selected brand dealer showroom.

What the research goes on to say is that almost no one (there are exceptions) will buy a car, sight-unseen and without "kicking the tyres". However, even though the brand website doesn't "sell" anything, its influence is still just as "mission critical".

General Motors in the US were one of the first car manufacturers to really understand the value of online. Inspired by examples from digital agency, Modem Media, GM created MyGM.gm.com. It was a place for the GM enthusiast to find out more about cars and get access to much more than you'd find on the basic website. You could register for news and invitations to special events and opportunities to drive the latest cars. It was also where the owner could register details of their own car, get reminders of services, get latest model upgrades and changes etc. It was one of the first very successful online

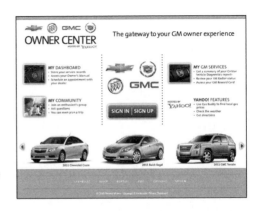

loyalty-driving programs which worked and, although a bit clunky in 1999, it won a lot of acclaim among GM target customers.

And GM has not given up on it! More than 11 years later, it still provides a strong community environment for GM owners.

Case study 5: Clothing

All the early research showed that clothing would be one of the least successful areas to go online. After all people really want to feel the cloth, see what it looks like, try it on, examine the fit, check it goes with other items. Buying clothes is a very visual, tactile and sensory buying experience. But, we have found that people do enjoy buying clothes online. And it's not just because it may be easier to find a special size but because it's convenient. And now indeed with Facebook you can find ways to share and explore shopping ideas with friends and get advice on what to buy (who needed MyFaveShop?). Here are just a few examples of how successful online clothing sales have become:

▷ Asos.com is an online fashion phenomenon. Its share price quadrupled in the space of just 18 months from its launch. It reaches customers all over the world, sales continue to increase at 20% to 30%-plus and profits at the last results announcement were up 59%.

▷ In China clothing led online retail growth in Q3 2010 (Interfax China).

▷ "Gap pins growth hopes on online and overseas sales." Glenn Murphy, CEO of Gap Inc., has stated that "our strong portfolio of brands combined with several powerful platforms such as outlet, online and franchise give us significant global runway" and announced plans to sell clothes online in Japan from 2011.

▷ From a piece of Deloitte research: "Consumers have been relatively slow to switch to buying clothes online but as retailers improve their website's visual merchandising and offer free and easy returns service this is changing fast. Clothing consumers in the 25 to 34 age group are the most multi-channel … This age group … tend to live their lives online via Smartphones and social networks." It comes as no surprise that a number of leading retail clothing groups launched Smartphone shopping apps in 2010.

▷ A piece of Google research found that, while tactility remains a purchase barrier for some, there is growing confidence in buying clothing online from trusted brands and especially for everyday wear such as shirts and repeat type purchases such as underwear.

What this success proves once and for all is that there are just no barriers to online success. Any product or service item can be made to work. It's just down to good old basic principles of understanding your market place and your customers and giving them what they want when they want it. Even fresh food is a growth sector in online shopping baskets and was the "fastest growing sector online for Tesco.com", albeit off a low base. In today's time-pressed world, time saved is highly valued.

Case study 6: Global law firm

If there are no limits on B2C, then what about the B2B arena? It's been argued that services which are complex, like legal services, are just not appropriate for an online world. Many lawyers felt that if a client wanted to decide which law firm to choose, or to get expert advice then that could only be done with face-to-face contact and building a personal relationship. In fact so arrogant were most law firms that they hardly bothered with a website and many just put up a token piece of brochureware. However, even law firms, no matter how high-end and sophisticated, have belatedly begun to realize that the online world might just be a little more important!

Here's an example from a top-10 global law firm. 2009 had seen profit pressures due to credit crunch fears and economic slow-down. Some redundancies had been made but mostly to ensure and protect levels of partner profitability, which remained high. In this context, the firm had not developed its online presence beyond a fairly basic website. But many in the law firm did not think that improving or investing in the site or more generally online would be worthwhile. "How many people visit the website and certainly how many would be influenced by it?" "Surely it was all about personal recommendations and personal networks, this online stuff had no relevance." And as for things like a strong presence on search engines or a social media strategy to engage with potential new staff trainees and associates from school, "Well, that was something for the likes of Coca-Cola, not us."

However, a new marketing director instinctively felt that the web had more influence and so some simple market research was conducted. "Let's go talk to our target customers and actually ask them, direct, whether they are influenced by what they see online." The answer that came back stunned the lawyers. After all, they don't expect to get things wrong. But the research findings were absolutely based on what their new target clients were saying. The message back from customers and clients was loud and clear and more or less unanimous:

> "For us, the web is the firm's window on the world ... it's the first place we go to rather than look at brochures or fancy white papers ... We expect a certain standard online, the kind of standard we'd expect from a top law firm ... if we don't see that then we're going to start wondering if what we see online reflects the quality of the advice we'll get offline."

"Yes, in something so personal and complex as legal advice we'd usually want to meet the firm and people we're going to work with … but when we're deciding on the pitch list we will do our due diligence and we find that starts with the website."

"We don't mind slick, we don't mind a bit cheesy but we do expect class."

"Yes, if I visited a firm's site and did not get a good and positive impression then it would change my mind about using them."

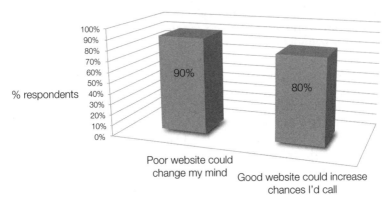

Figure 13   **How the quality of a website affects customers' attitudes**

The anecdotal feedback on how the quality of the website affected potential customers' attitudes was confirmed by survey data, and the results were equally alarming (Figure 13).

The firm's website was appalling. The home page, for example, featured an interview which was nearly 2 years old between a partner who'd subsequently left the firm and a client who was so obscure they sounded like a small local doughnut company. Practice areas often had no content and it was sometimes hard to see if the firm had any expertise in its listed areas of activity. Worse still, it was hard to find how to contact the firm, who to contact and their phone number. And when, eventually, it was possible to find an email address, it was a generic info@ address. That might have been ok because it promised next-day response, but the info@ inbox was rarely checked so genuine enquiries from prospective new clients usually went unanswered!

And while the new staff/careers section was a bit more dynamic and up-to-date, it had little information and the key social websites for aspiring lawyers like RollonFriday and LawCareers carried content from most of the rival firms but nothing from this one.

The list of site negatives went on and on. It was only when the senior partner group saw the hard evidence that they finally agreed (still somewhat reluctantly) to invest in a site update and revitalized online presence. And here is a firm with a turnover of more than £1bn and individual partner profit at around £400k (no debt and very cash flow positive) hesitating about spending around £500k on an investment which their prospective clients are saying is the item that most influences their initial selection!

What they had not realized was just how quickly online information and presentation had become engrained and entrenched and how business habits had changed so fast that the proverbial "tipping point" had been reached. Old-fashioned networks and traditional contacts had not been displaced but they had been added to, and in a material way. Client selection was now "multi-channel" and certainly contained an important digital information component. This had become vital but the lawyers, immersed in their day-to-day arcane world, had not realized it. They needed a wake-up call!

This situation is not that untypical. There remains the view that the real B2B activity is still done via a sales force with face-to-face contact and people who build long-term relationships. And there is nothing wrong with that. But most customers, as the law firm found out, are starting to expect more and more online information. And they expect that it will be smartly presented. It's "the face of the firm" to the outside world. They expect extranet facilities where they can check on progress of any joint activities. They expect My Account features so they can look at purchase history, invoice status, payment and receipts. They expect special news updates which are relevant to them and their business. They want content and site material configured for use on their iPad and iPhone, they demand an excellent search facility that lets them find exactly what they want quickly and easily. If Company X is not offering these sorts of tools and functions then, for sure, there's a Company Y knocking on the door with just these initiatives.

Case study 7: Other B2B examples

▷ HP: a good site with lots of information and links but a contact phone number that only works Monday to Friday, 9 to 5. It's another example of an old-fashioned approach. In the "good old days", customers had no expectation of being able to do business outside of weekdays, 9 to 5. But today's world is all about the "convenience of now". We want to be able to contact, discover, communicate, organize meetings and network at a time that suits us. We may be overseas, we may be discussing business partners with our colleagues and deciding who to shortlist or call. We expect 24/7 access and response.

▷ Cisco.com: a very good example of a strong B2B-focused website. There is clear product and service information on the site, a multi-channel contact strategy with call centre and partner locator by region, support documentation and video guides, listings of training, events and professional certification, webcasts and seminars, a "My Cisco" account centre for customers which is the privileged access and content area, plus a How to Buy call to action. It works. It's their fifth-generation website and continues to evolve and improve. It sits alongside a broad and strong web presence which includes a solid search engine first-page presence and clear viral social networking policy. Cisco can be followed on YouTube at YouTube.com/user/Cisco, they have their own blogs at http://blogs.cisco.com, there is the Cisco Networking academy on Facebook as well as separate Cisco Retail and Cisco Systems Facebook pages proudly proclaiming that they've now reached over 100,000 "likes", there is a Cisco "superfan" program to promote positive influencers and networkers, there's a "tourguide" on an official Twitter feed and there are additional Twitter-based initiatives on CiscoLiveEurope and CiscoSystems.

Every company needs its seminal moment or wake-up call. For Cisco it came some years ago. They did their annual sales analysis, looking at who had been their biggest customers and they suddenly realized that one of them, who had done some $100m of business with them that year, had in fact never received a sales call or sales rep visit. Immediately the traditional reactions kicked in: this is a big customer, let's arrange a high level meeting, we can talk long-term strategy and extended product sales. But when they called to set things up they were told: love the products, love the support but we like to do business online and we'd like to stick with that. Just keep updating the website!

▷ Specialist traders: There have for some years now been a very developed set of global trading websites which manage a growing share of world trade in exports and imports. Alibaba.com regularly wins awards for best global B2B site as it seeks to match buyers and sellers across a wide range of products from chemicals, agricultural equipment, commodities and ingredients to olive oil, apples and all the way through to fashion accessories. It's the world's best bazaar! Other sites have more specialist regional or product focus, for example, TradeIndia and TradeEgypt or ResearchChemicalsOnline.

* * * * *

All the evidence from these case studies simply recognizes that the web does play an extraordinary part in B2B commerce, whether it's directly selling or influencing the sale or extending a Brand's reach and business development potential. Now B2B is getting much more attention. Google was voted "best B2B brand of 2010", beating out Apple.com/Business, Office Depot, Viking Direct, Experian.com and AccountancyAge.com. Each of these had recently rebuilt and established clear actionable B2B websites with extended web presence through a selected mix of campaigns, search marketing excellence, social media activity and connected multi-channel contact programs.

A 2011 "brand health check" carried out by Havas showed that those companies which demonstrated excellence online, the vanguard companies, are still, despite all the case studies, a minority! In their research, spanning over 30,000 people across 4 continents, they found that only 30% of today's largest Brands were considered to have "a meaningful and relevant online presence". And when asked to consider the consequences of that, most of the respondents said that if the brand had no engagement online then they would just go to a rival brand or company that did!

Many Brands are still not living up to expectations or to standards set by leading organizations: "Digital and indirect communications are becoming pivotal platforms for brands to fuel the dialogue, engage customers and build trust ... There's a real opportunity for companies who shift from relying on 'what they do' [i.e. traditional marketing] ... to start building relevant brand roles and engaging initiatives that capture the 'collective will' and spur people into action."

These "Brand Health" checks by the likes of Havas are becoming ever more popular and here's a basic checklist to assess a Brand's modern relevance and sustainability:

---

1   *Find out where your customers are connecting with your Brand.* That's the kind of brand audit and "buzz monitoring" discussed previously (c.f. Chapter 5).

2   *Understand how customers are using the web.* What are they looking for when they search? Is it product details? Do they want to browse and research or are they looking to buy? Is it after-sales service, maintenance contracts, complaints or returns, contact details etc? All this can be discovered through basic web analysis packages that monitor page views and visits, dwell times and drop-off points. And it can be supplemented with basic customer research, whether a one-off evening focus group, a quick online survey (e.g. SurveyMonkey.com) or more detailed Havas-type global research.

3   *What is today's perception of the Brand?* Again the buzz monitoring and sentiment indices alongside any supplemental research can immediately identify strengths and weaknesses.

4   *What are key competitors up to?* If you take most B2C products and services there is a huge amount of investment, improvement and learning taking place, and there is just no room for inaction, under-investment or complacency. The B2B world has also experienced waves of innovation although, as our law firm found, it's been possible to get away with doing nothing until now!

5   *Recognize the social media shift and that customers now do have more control over the brand's future.* A strong, vigorous, proactive and adequately funded and resourced social media strategy and plan is critical for this coming decade. Just setting up a page on Facebook is not the answer! Chapter 8 on social media also explores the potential upsides of getting this right.

16 UK Case Study:
The Benefits of Going Digital

It's exciting to think and speculate about our future world, but there's hard work to be done to get there. What we do know is that there's an amazing and world-wide platform that has already been established, and in a very short amount of time. A recent BCG/Google study looked at how the global internet economy was developing and considered its potential. It used the UK as an example because it is in some ways the most developed in the world.

It found that the internet contributed an estimated £100 billion or 7.2% of GDP to the UK economy. That GDP share is larger than the country's construction, transportation and utilities industries combined. It grew from relatively nothing in just 10 years.

Indeed the internet has become so important for the UK that it is a net exporter of e-commerce goods and services, exporting £2.80 for every £1 imported. It also contributes to price stabilization and even price deflation by enabling intensive product pricing comparison and competition. Cost savings are estimated at about £18 billion or close to £1000 per online household annually.

Comparing the UK internet economy with those of other countries, the UK comes out well-placed, being ranked as the 6th most intensively developed e-economy in the world. It is the largest in terms of absolute spend per household. It is also the largest in terms of absolute billions of GDP, ahead of Germany, which is 9th, and the US, which is 11th.

The rankings are based on three factors which take account of GDP and spend but also consider other items:

1 "Enablement": how well built is the infrastructure and how available is the access?
2 Expenditure: how much are consumers and businesses spending online?
3 Engagement: how actively are businesses, government and consumers embracing the Net?

In terms of *Enablement*, the UK still has some way to go to fulfill its potential. It ranks 23 on this measure in terms of average household broadband speed with only 15% of households having connections above 5 megabytes per second. That contrasts with, for example, Korea at 65%, Japan at 60%,

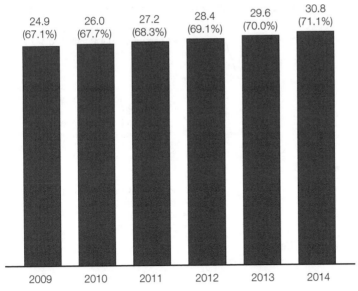

Note: ages 14+; buy monthly

Figure 14   **UK online buyers and penetration, 2009–2014, millions and percentage of internet users**
Source: eMarketer.

40% in Scandinavia and 25% in the US. And there is plenty of evidence to show that as average speeds grow so time spent on the Net increases.

In terms of *Expenditure*, the UK emerged as the top nation with the highest per capita spending online. In fact this spend figure is probably a very conservative estimate to quantify the value of this sector. But it shows that some 26 million people, which is nearly half the country's population, bought travel, goods or other services online in 2010, spending roughly £1,600 per person (Figure 14).

In terms of *Engagement*, in a recent study by Synovate, some 92% of people in the UK said they now could not live without the internet (compared with 90% of Spaniards, 89% of Americans and, surprisingly, as many as 70% of all Chinese): "the internet is ... tightly woven into everyday lives ... [it] is embedded in Brit's lives."

"Engagement" also investigated the "ripple effect" – the ever-widening benefit of continued investment and government support illustrated in Figure 15. If a country can achieve "centre of excellence" status then it will inevitably encourage a wider range of supporting businesses to start up and flourish. One supplier has a knock-on effect throughout an industry value chain. Indeed, this was a theme most compellingly advanced by Michael Porter in his ground-breaking book *The Competitive Advantage of Nations*. In that, he convincingly demonstrated that where one country had achieved success in a sector – take, for example, the global leadership of the Financial

Only some of the internet's impacts on the UK economy are captured by GDP

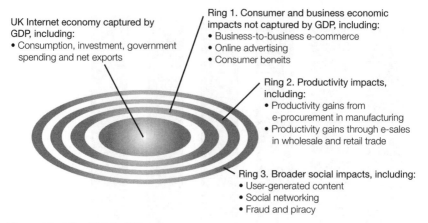

UK Internet economy captured by GDP, including:
- Consumption, investment, government spending and net exports

Ring 1. Consumer and business economic impacts not captured by GDP, including:
- Business-to-business e-commerce
- Online advertising
- Consumer beneits

Ring 2. Productivity impacts, including:
- Productivity gains from e-procurement in manufacturing
- Productivity gains through e-sales in wholesale and retail trade

Ring 3. Broader social impacts, including:
- User-generated content
- Social networking
- Fraud and piracy

Figure 15   **The Ripple Effect**
Source: The Boston Consulting Group: The Connected Kingdom.

Services sector in London – then if government specifically protects and supports that sector, not surprisingly, it will breed further success. But, as Porter pointed out, it was also surprising how often governments did *not* move to protect their "golden geese" and neglect inevitably allows other nations to establish rival and ultimately better centers of excellence.

So the UK has an opportunity to establish a global leadership position where the "ripple effects" can bring a wide range of benefits to the economy. European Union research in 2010 went further and tried to quantify these benefits in terms of expected contribution to employment and competitiveness. Their research suggested:

▷ a 10% total increase in investment in online capability in one region can lead to a 1% to 2% increase in employment in that local business community,

▷ a 10% increase in e-procurement activity can lead to a 2.6% increase in productivity; and the potential is greater if it covers the whole supply chain because that can result in lower prices and increased competitiveness,

▷ a 10% increase in online sales can lead to a 3.1% increase in productivity by more efficient use of selling and other traditional distribution costs,

▷ a 10% increase in number of employees with personal access to high speed broadband can raise productivity and speed of response by 1%.

Leading e-business economies today therefore have a wonderful opportunity to build on and develop their digital technology leadership. As we move towards 2020 that will increasingly become the main driver of growth and competitiveness, and it will be those centers that actively mix government support and initiative with private sector investment and bold leadership which will have the potential to be future winners.

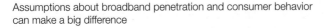

Assumptions about broadband penetration and consumer behavior can make a big difference

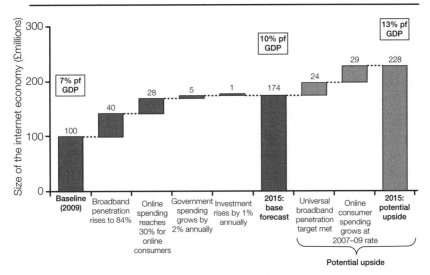

Sources: AllianceBernstein; Economist Intelligence Unit; European Commission; IMRG; Gartner; International Telecommunications Office; UK Office for National Statistics; Ovum/Datamonitor; BCG analysis.
Note: Some amounts may not add up to the numbers shown because of rounding.

Figure 16   **Forecast internet contribution to UK GDP by 2015**
Source: The Boston Consulting Group: The Connected Kingdom.

And if they achieve that, what can they expect? In their study, BCG looked out till 2015. They saw continued and significant growth for the internet economy globally (Figure 16). In the UK specifically, they forecast growth potentially up to 13% of GDP by 2015. That's nearly double the 2010 percentage in just 5 years, to nearly £200 billion. And at 13%, it would make the internet economy bigger than the UK Financial Services sector.

What will drive this? As Figure 16 shows, there are a number of key factors which will be influential as every country looks out to the development of its online economy:

(i)   The quality of the broadband infrastructure enabling fast transmission of data.
(ii) An infrastructure which is "rock solid" and reliable.
(iii) An infrastructure which reaches all households. (In the UK this is currently very dependent on BT's own investment capabilities and timetable.)
(iv) Continued consumer shift in the way they purchase and the proportion of goods and services that are purchased online.
(v)   Continued shift in the way media and content is consumed.
(vi) Developments in mobile access and, for example, small-value item Payforit services.

(vii)   Continued innovation among existing and potential new suppliers. For example, who will be the next breakthrough digital and online innovators, like Lovefilm/Netflix disrupting traditional store-based film rental? Who will be the next Comparethemarket.com or the next Cheapflights.com?

(viii) Open source access, which has been the key in fuelling smart phone take-up such as the open access/structured supplier developer program for the Apple API (application programming interface), for example. This does away with the old and limiting "walled garden" approach (even though most Mobile Network Operators still try to direct consumers to their own controlled content zones).

(ix)   Device functionality and ease of use which allows new ways of accessing and leveraging digital technology, for example, the suite of products from Apple: iPod, iPhone and iPad.

(x)   And finally, consumer confidence. This includes the confidence to try new devices and new ways of doing things (for example, fears about personal data security slowed online buying behavior for several years till consumers reached an assurance point that it was no more of an issue online than offline). Consumer confidence also includes the confidence to spend. In times of recessions and down-turns, government pressure to cut investment and spending and fear of job losses will slow this down.

Matt Brittin, the CEO in the UK of Google, has tried to sum up this future potential:

> We all know how the Internet has changed the way people access information and communicate ... Now for the first time we can see how its adoption by British business has become a major contributor to GDP ... The sector has come of age and with great prospects for further growth the Internet economy will be vital to future prosperity.

And as an article in *Computer Weekly* warned, you ignore it at your peril!

17 Case Study: How the Cloud Facilitates the Technology Solution

According to the US National Science Foundation, the number of internet users, further enabled by mobile access, will rise from the present 1.7 billion to 5 billion by 2020. That would suggest that the vast majority of households in the world will have some form of internet connection. All this predicted growth is also generating a lot of digital data. Perhaps slightly disturbingly, the amount of data and content that will need to be stored and processed is growing exponentially.

For companies looking to adapt and evolve to transform for the digital age there is clearly a substantial challenge. And if they are to truly get to grips with the 2020 world then it's not only about the vision and structures and processes and skills, but it will also be about how they get to grips with all the data so it becomes useful and can be integrated into more informed real-time decision-making

In 2010, the size of the world's total digital content was estimated in a CIO.com paper at 500 billion gigabytes or 500 exabytes. (An exabyte is the unit of information or computer storage that is equal to: 1,000,000,000,000,000,000 bytes, which is the same as 1 billion gigabytes or 1 million terabytes.) So when the University of Berkeley California announced in 1999 that "all words ever spoken by human beings could be stored in approximately 5 exabytes of data", they were – surprise, surprise – completely underestimating the human capacity to generate stuff. In a subsequent study just three years later, the University found that all the telephone calls made in 2002 on land lines and mobiles would contain 17.3 exabytes of new information if stored in a digital form. And in 2006, the IDC estimated that 160 exabytes of digital information were created and captured worldwide. By 2013, annual global IP traffic is expected to reach 667 exabytes (which for those who really want to know is getting close to 1 zetabyte!)

As IBM have put it: "Data analysis and information used to be a river ... Today, it's a roiling ocean of data, constantly expanding its shores ... in just 4 years from now [2015], the amount of digital information in the world will double every 11 hours." And as IBM go on so succinctly: "It can be a daunting task for any enterprise to try to sift through and undertake massive data analysis, extracting information and transforming it into action-able knowledge."

The key enabler of this extraordinary growth is what Gordon Moore fore-saw when working at Intel as far back as 1965. In what has now famously become known as 'Moore's Law', he predicted that the number of transis-tors that could be placed on an integrated circuit would double every two years. Amazingly, this trend has now continued for 46 years and is expected to carry on till at least 2015. This is having a huge impact on processing speed, memory capacity, device size and cost. It is powering the acceptance and development of the digital economy. It is enabling more and more data to be easily captured and stored. And while Moore himself now doubts how long this can continue after 2015, there are constantly new breakthroughs in chip technology. (The latest ideas involve nanotechnology techniques.) At the time of writing, this general trend is expected to continue. According to a report on ZDNet, we have another 10 to 20 years at least in the pipeline and in the lab before we reach the fundamental barrier that is the size of the atom. Perhaps by then we'll have cracked that one too.

So the advent of "cloud computing" is timely in providing some help to manage this potential data overload. In principle it enables an organization to more easily store and access data remotely. It also allows the company to rent or buy other people's software and hardware tools and innovations on an as-needs basis. You no longer have to build it all yourself! "The Cloud" provides opportunities for companies to establish a virtual infrastructure, to take advantage of next-generation software solutions *without* having to de-velop your own and go through complex integration. It cuts costs dramati-cally, removes the risk of expensive IT investment that often doesn't work as planned and significantly reduces time to market.

Figure 17 shows a good example of widespread impact of the Cloud.

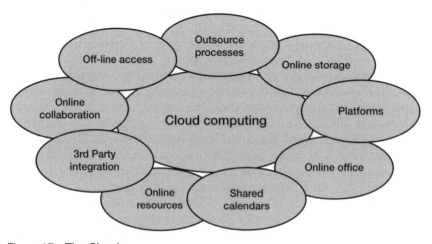

Figure 17   **The Cloud**
Source: IBM.

Taken from an interview by BBC's Tim Weber, we can look at how Rentokil have taken advantage of Cloud-based solutions. Rentokil International is a global business services group that employs 68,000 people across 50 countries. It had an email environment which consisted of 40 different systems across different operating units and acquired organizations. They quite naturally wanted to consolidate that system into one. One option was to hire, for example, IBM to establish a global server infrastructure – a system that would have been very high-cost and taken some time to implement. But with the new "cloud computing" environment, Rentokil were able to quickly roll out Google's enterprise email across the company. It was 70% less expensive and ongoing support costs are also low.

In effect Rentokil are renting space on Google servers, a kind of "IT as a service" or "software as a service" (SaaS) as it's now frequently called, providing access to data and software over the internet. This is ideal, especially for workforces which are heavily dispersed across the globe such as Rentokil's. They can now access their emails at any time through any web browser. Meantime, the costs of hardware and software maintenance and upgrades lie with the provider.

Information technology starts to become a utility and therein lies the strength and power of this "cloud" development. It can be consumed like electricity or water and, in effect, fully outsourced.

Of course such a way of working is not really that new. Services like Hotmail, Flickr and Facebook all operate in the same way. Ventures such as Salesforce.com, set up in 2000, provided early versions of the "Cloud". (Why invest in an expensive Oracle Siebel enterprise implementation program when you can "rent"/pay as you go for all the functionality you will need?)

But now businesses big and small are seeing this opportunity to significantly improve their technology environment without the big project risks and costs involved. Companies like Aviva, the global insurance provider, have moved all their enterprise content, management and business intelligence tools online and they have gone to Microsoft's Sharepoint to access that capability and service. Logistics company, Pall-Ex, has moved much of its IT to a UK hosting firm called Outsourcery. Universal Music is using the cloud computing service of Venda, the e-commerce solutions business, to set up its online stores across Europe. It's so expensive to build a world class e-commerce platform, no single retailer can build it by themselves unless they are the size of Amazon," says James Cronin of Venda. So why do that when it can simply be provided and white-labelled by another company?

And as more and more realize the potential of the cloud using digital technology tools, so it will fuel further growth and development on the supply side, providing better customer applications and service(s) and encouraging further demand-side activity. The Cloud is encouraging a major shift in computing. "Social computing will be the 'defining concept' for the industry," says Marc Benioff, the founder of Salesforce.com. Olof Schroeder of Microsoft agrees: "People are working more and more from everywhere … home and workspace are merging." By using Cloud services, people have access to the same facilities and functionalities wherever they are. If they can get email anywhere then why not get everything else as well, rather than having to wait to get back to the office? One of the issues with the Cloud has been data security, and opinion is still divided. According to Casio Dreyfuss at Gartner, there are "enormous security ... and auditing risks that have not been addressed yet," but Google's Dave Girouard is more positive, saying that Cloud computing "has a good track record." He goes on to comment : "Cloud computing is just at the start of its evolution.". On this, Casio Dreyfuss agrees: "All business computing will be more web-enabled. For some [companies] it will reach the point where it will be totally web-centric."

* * * * *

The internet future and the digital technology world is an exciting one. It's already well-established and the fact that it contributes so much today to GDP and has so much economic potential in the future shows just how pervasive and unstoppable is its reach and momentum. Many companies in the first part of this decade are under pressure to manage budgets and investment conservatively, but it will be hard to resist the lure of digital technology innovation as that is driving all the growth and will be the core source of competitive advantage into the future.

Index

Acknowledgments

The author and publishers would like to thank the following for permission to use various images, charts and data that provide example and illustration in this book:

The Boston Consulting Group for charts about the Internet economy, IBM for their representation of the Cloud, ITU for the chart on most and least connected countries, eMarketer for their chart on UK internet penetration, Imtiaz Khaderbhoy for the digital crossroads image, News International for their images and information, FutureSource Consulting for Europe household data forecasts, Digital Surgeons for their Facebook vs. Twitter analysis and graphic, Mike Fruchter for his mobile phone apps image, Pingdom for their chart on tech company assets, Emotiv for the Emotiv EPOC neuro headset, the IAB UK and USA for their charts on internet usage and expenditures, Gesture Cube for the remote sensor image and Lunar Europe for the design, McKinsey & Co for the 7S model framework, Radian 6 for their web analytics compilation, Ross Dawson and Future Exploration for the future of the newspaper industry graphic and finally Rob Jenkins for his designs and graphics on the roadmap, global migration and multi-channel mobile+cart.

Every effort has been made to contact all the copyright-holders, but if any have been inadvertently overlooked the publishers will be pleased to make the necessary arrangements at the first opportunity.